It's Comeback Time!

"Personal Forecast" Strategies To Overcome Set-backs

by

Ron Craycraft

Copyright © 2008 by Ron Craycraft

It's Comeback Time!
by Ron Craycraft

www.ForecastForLife.org

Ron Craycraft
Senior Pastor, Author

Printed in the United States of America

ISBN 978-1-60647-971-1

All rights reserved solely by the author. The author guarantees all contents are original and do not infringe upon the legal rights of any other person or work. No part of this book may be reproduced in any form without the permission of the author. The views expressed in this book are not necessarily those of the publisher.

All Scripture quotations are taken from the New King James Version.
Copyright © 1982 by Thomas Nelson, Inc.
Used by permission. All rights reserved.

The *"storms of life"* will threaten to
"rock your world."
But your *personal forecast* of God's Word
will bring hope, healing, faith, love, peace,
and victory through Christ.

www.xulonpress.com

Contents

PERSONAL FORECAST STRATEGY 1
Stir Yourself Up! 9

PERSONAL FORECAST STRATEGY 2
Take It By Force! 19

PERSONAL FORECAST STRATEGY 3
How To Walk On Water 33

PERSONAL FORECAST STRATEGY 4
Who's The Boss? 45

PERSONAL FORECAST STRATEGY 5
Activate the Power of the Holy Spirit............63

PERSONAL FORECAST STRATEGY 6
Cure For the Common *Cold — Heart* 79

PERSONAL FORECAST STRATEGY 7
You Are the Prophet In Your Own Life......... 97

PERSONAL FORECAST STRATEGY 8
The Word Will Make You Free 111

90 Powerful Forecast Confessions 129

****

Have life's challenges made you feel
like you are losing it?
Does it feel like you are losing *big time* at halftime?
Have you had disappointment and discouragement?

Are you addicted to anything?
Are you lonely, sick, or depressed?

Do you need to *break free* from past hurts?

Do you need to *break free* from worry,
confusion, sorrow, or fear?

Have you ever thought
that you have no real purpose in life?
You can rebound from defeat.
You can break free from bondage.
You can make a comeback from every setback!

****
It's Comeback Time!
****

PERSONAL FORECAST STRATEGY 1

Stir Yourself Up!
(It's "Comeback" Time – Decision Time)

One day it became very clear to me that I was going to die—and very soon!

I knew exactly what I had to do before it was too late, but I just couldn't *stir up* enough desire to do anything about it.

I felt trapped, condemned, and addicted—but also strangely satisfied to just *hide away* from my feelings, troubles, and disappointments. Alcohol became my "counterfeit" secret hiding place from the *"cares of this world."* As strange as it might sound, I also felt a certain amount of comfort and consolation with my new substitute friends: "depression and self-pity."

I'm embarrassed to say it—but at that point in my life I didn't even *want to* quit hiding out.

Destiny Sabotage

Some of us have sabotaged our own future. We have experienced the goodness and protection of God but allowed some kind of compromise to tear a hole in that hedge of protection.

That was me. I allowed the "cares of this world" to establish a stronghold—and it seemed like I was looking for some kind of quick relief. I chose the wrong thing. I began to hide alcohol in the garage, in the cupboards, under the bed, and in closets—it was an every day quest.

Some people who hear my story think that it couldn't have been that bad. Let me be vividly open and honest. There were days when I had the shakes and hallucinated so much that I couldn't write my signature or even walk. Enough said?

As you can see, I am not referring to just a socially acceptable sin. I ended up with all the classic symptoms. Miraculously I avoided jail and losing my job. *(It is true—God's grace cannot be explained; it certainly was not deserved.)*

I allowed depression and addiction to alcohol to enter my soul, and it almost claimed my life. My entire future was in jeopardy, along with the rest of my family.

My testimony and my body were damaged. I surrendered to a spirit of depression, and I lost my zeal to encourage others toward the abundant life of Christ. My own heart condemned me. The devil took advantage—and held me hostage.

Too Condemned To Pray

At my lowest point—at the doorway of alcohol poison and certain death—*(when I couldn't even pray)*—I began to look beyond the guilt and circumstances to simply confess Bible promises. The Holy Spirit soon planted a special word in my heart: *"forecast."*

The word *"forecast"* became my glimmer of hope. I knew I didn't have the "natural guts" to quit what I was doing on my own. But this word, *"forecast"* gave me a jolt of energy. It was like an opening in a darkened sky when just a faint ray of sunlight gets through.

Suddenly I could look beyond my miserable circumstances and begin to speak with a fresh positive faith in Bible promises. Physically I couldn't see anything happening yet. But I had God's promises that His Word will always accomplish His Will. (Isaiah 55:11.) I suddenly sensed a break free moment, and began to see with "eyes of faith." *(Sometimes we can see more with our physical eyes closed.)*

The "comeback" started with the familiar Scripture, *"I can do all things through Christ Who strengthens me"*—and the *"I will not be defeated"* prayers of my wife, family, and friends. I began to quietly read "out-loud" the "I can do" Scripture. Then more Scripture confessions were added to a list of more than 100 *personal forecasts* of faith.

At first glance many sincere Christians miss this vitally important solution. *(It seems too easy to have that much power.)* I've heard the old phrases for years, *"read your Bible and pray every day."* But I let the devil deceive me into *skipping over* this seemingly "too simple" answer.

Praying the Word of God *with Holy Spirit power* is always God's best plan for our break free victories and making a *"Comeback."*

Grace and Healing

I could ramble on with many detailed excuses, (circumstances and family history), but I'm not going any further with the grisly details. The truth is that my Word level was on empty. I became spiritually weak. It's like starving to death because of needing food and water. My "spiritman" was starving for the Word of God—so I had weak faith and zero resistance.

Let's just say that God's law of sowing and reaping is always in effect on planet Earth. If you do things the Bible says not to do—you allow the world's curses to enter your life.

Resist! Begin to feed yourself good spiritual "faith food" (God's Word), listen for the silent leading of the Holy Spirit, and pray in the "mighty name of Jesus." *(It will also be an added benefit to" take in" good physical food and water, with daily exercise.)*

Now if you think that everything happens for a reason and God wanted me to go through this to teach me something—you're wrong. I already know that God is good and is not responsible for my sin at all. It was not God's will, but He had mercy.

I could spend several chapters relating the dozens of Scriptures from God's Word about the sins that cause our future to be cursed (unbelief, ungodliness, drunkenness, gluttony, gossip, complaining, murmuring and verbal abuses). But let's move on. Let's move toward a better future in Christ Jesus.

"Forgetting those things which are behind and reaching forward to those things which are ahead, I press toward the goal for the prize of the upward call of God in Christ Jesus"
                                                    Philippians 3:13-14

My confession of sin has been done in severe agony, and my repentance has been a painful process. But the Lord was always waiting to supply His healing grace whenever I was ready to surrender. *(The repentance took a long time, but the Lord's grace and healing came to me instantaneously when I submitted my life to His Word of promise.)*

Celebrate Victory "In Christ"

Something discouraging happens to me every day. Does that surprise you?

Minor discouraging events sometimes come to me in bunches. It could start with something as simple as a comment or complaint from someone I meet during the day.

If I don't deal with the source "head on" by faith in God's promises—I will end up with the natural flow of negative, ungodly results. I might even *give up* on something I've been praying and believing God to do in my life. If I don't resist the negative emotions and recharge myself with the "Spirit and Word" of Christ—a lingering depression can potentially steal my joy, peace, faith, hope, finances, and health for long periods of time.

You might be thinking, *"Yes, that's me too! I've been stuck in a negative, unfulfilled, 'down-in-the-dumps' mode for quite a while."*

People who are not aggressively "living by faith" every day, have a natural tendency to get spiritually weak, make wrong decisions, and resort to "covering up" hurts with hate, revenge, alcohol, gambling, drugs, having a *pity party*, overeating, power shopping, or other destructive behaviors.

The saddest thing is that even people with an established godly purpose in life can get sidetracked and "give up" on their Spirit-led dream when confronted with an attack of the enemy.

But there's a way to overcome! There are easy steps you can take that will bring help from heaven to override negative attitudes and circumstances.

With the unfailing, life-changing Word of God and powerful strength from the Holy Spirit, you can become a prophet in your own life!—and build your own victorious "Comeback Celebration."

You Can Begin Again

Now it's your time to make a *forecast* of victory!

You might be thinking, *"I don't have a comeback story to celebrate."* (You might have one "waiting in the wings" that you just don't see yet.)

Hopefully you have not fallen for the trap of addiction.

But let me ask you to "examine" your heart and life—you might already know of something you should get victory over, and give praise honor and glory to the Lord for helping you escape.

Are you trapped by worry, doubt, and fear?

Are you allowing grief or sorrow about the past to hold you hostage?

Are you disappointed, discouraged, or discontented?

For some people it's a stronghold of worry—for some it's a sense of failure, or lack of accomplishment—for others it's a selfish, "whatever makes me feel good" dead-end lifestyle.

You are divinely destined to be like Jesus and imitate His *faith attitude*. What would Jesus do? He would pray and speak a Scripture—just like He did when confronted by the devil in Mark, chapter 4.

Jesus would give thanks and praise to the heavenly Father, in advance of what He saw with His physical eyes.

Most believers stagger at that thought. They are overly aware of their own natural failures and shortcomings. They feel unequipped and inadequate to tell others about their victories in Christ.

The fact is we *are* equipped. Ephesians 1 says so. It tells that the God and Father of our Lord Jesus Christ has already blessed us.

"Blessed be the God and Father of our Lord Jesus Christ, who has blessed us with every spiritual blessing in the heavenly places in Christ, just as He chose us in Him before the foundation of the world, that we should be holy and without blame before Him in love"

Ephesians 1: 3-5

Think of it! God gave you everything necessary to be holy and blameless before Him. He set aside *for you* all the blessings and divine power it would take *for you* to represent Him on the earth and bring praise and glory to the name of Jesus.

> *"According to the good pleasure of His will, to the praise of the glory of His grace, by which He made us accepted in the Beloved"*
>
> Ephesians 1:5b-6

You might look at yourself and wonder why God would ever think you could be like Him at all? I'll tell you why. God knew you before you ever sinned. He knew you to be wonderful. He knew you before your life got messed up. He knew you before the devil ever got his hands on you. God has given you and I the chance to begin again.

Every day is a chance to celebrate a new "comeback!"

Stir Up the Gift of God

There is life-changing power in learning to forget the hurts of the past. Actually, we will not fully enjoy the victory that belongs to us as born-again children of God until we learn how to supernaturally forget.

If you are like me, you can probably make a long list of things that you wish you would have not done in your life. But the Lord Jesus is always interceding for you to forget the past and look forward to your purpose in life. *(We cannot change the past—we cannot even change what happened 5 minutes ago. Even the angels from heaven can't change the past!)*

The apostle Paul, who had many opportunities to quit and "give up" continued to encourage other Christians and even pastors.

> *"Therefore I remind you to stir up the gift of God which is in you through the laying on of my hands. For God has not given us a spirit of fear, but of power and of love and of a sound mind"*
>
> 2 Timothy 1:6-7

You have a divinely planned purpose in this life. We need to start believing and receiving that Bible truth today!

> *"For I know the thoughts that I think toward you, says the LORD, thoughts of peace and not of evil, to give you a future and a hope"*
>
> Jeremiah 29:11

I know sometimes that's hard to believe when you're up to your eyeballs in the daily demands of living. When it's all you can do just to deal with the bills—and the kids—and the job, life can seem anything but divine. You can be tempted to wonder if you're destined to be or do anything truly great. You can be tempted to decide that even if you had such a destiny, you just don't have what it takes to fulfill it.

It is absolutely vital that you resist those thoughts and temptations.

Why? Because the Lord is "cheering" for you to make a victory comeback. The Lord is faithful and pleased to see us overcome and bounce back from life's setbacks.

Just like a sports team that is labeled as the "underdog," the faithful fans are thrilled to see their team win—especially when the experts thought they should not even be in the game.

There are people in this world who will never know the lord Jesus unless they hear your testimony—and realize that they can make a comeback too!

If You're Not Growing in Faith, You'll Slip Backward

These are serious days. It's no time to be sitting on the fence and being double-minded. We can *decide* where we are going to give our time—where we are going to put our trust.

Dependence on God requires spending time with Him and His Word, because faith comes by hearing and hearing by the Word of God. By spending time in the Word, we will become fully persuaded that God is faithful. This assurance gives peace and replaces every fear.

Fifty years ago no one would have thought biological weapons and epidemic diseases would be a threat today. But we have the antidote! God will deliver us when we abide in Him, trust Him and say so.

When you hear threatening reports, talk back! Say, *"No, that's not coming to me, or to my house!"* Don't let the enemy talk you out of your healing and protection. Receive all the good things God has declared for you in Psalm 91.

Be An Overcomer

As long as we are living in this world, there will be challenges to overcome.

Jesus Himself said we would have tribulation in this world. But the good news is that He has already overcome the world!

> *"These things I have spoken to you, that in Me you may have peace. In the world you will have tribulation; but be of good cheer, I have overcome the world"*
> John 16:33

You might be thinking, *"Well, that's great for Him—but what about me?"*

The answer is easy.

When you are born again— believing and confessing that Jesus is your Lord and Savior—you are now "in Christ." When you are "in Christ," you have His Word, His authority, and the Holy Spirit to help you overcome the world too!

> *"For whatever is born of God overcomes the world. And this is the victory that has overcome the world—our faith"*
> 1 John 5:4

Now you might be thinking, *"That sounds great—but how do I do that?"*

This answer is not so easy.

The answer to this "how to" question is exactly what this book is about: *"How to" overcome and rise above problems, hurts, addictions, and challenges with the "Word and Spirit" of Christ Jesus.*

Celebrate Your Courageous Victories!

You might be a homemaker who is depressed and exhausted. You might be a minister who is discouraged and overworked. You may have recently lost a loved one. You might be a business person who has financial challenges. Or, you might be an employee who has been demoted, laid off, or stressed out.

Everyone has "something" that needs to be completed, corrected, resisted, healed, or overcome. Even your favorite pastor, teacher, or TV star has challenges and discouragements that have to be overcome with courage.

A dictionary definition of "courage" is, "the mental or moral strength and tenacity to resist opposition, danger, or hardship." A Bible definition of *courage* is similar, but with one big exception. Bible courage is far more powerful because it is not with our own limited strength, but with the awesome strength of the "Spirit of Christ."

Spiritually speaking, if we are born again, we are complete in Christ Jesus. We are blessed with every spiritual blessing in heavenly places. But as long as we are still "in" our earth clothes—(and have to deal with an enemy who is always trying to feed us wrong thinking, condemnation, and discouragement)—we will be fighting the *good fight of faith* and casting down temptations, complacency, or addictive behavior.

That is why I say that we are all building our own *"comeback"* story!

Because of the great fall of mankind from the presence of God in the Garden of Eden, *"we all"* have a *"comeback"* story!

I don't know about you, but I need a daily refreshing and recharging of Holy Spirit power every day. I need to continue and comeback to a daily fellowship with Christ and His Word. We all make our journey through life *"in fellowship"* with God, our

Creator—or *"out of fellowship"* with God, our Creator. *"In"* is better!

You might be thinking, *"I've been stuck in a rut for way too long." "Why can't I change?"*

People want to change, but they're stuck. *"It's Comeback Time"* will help anyone get unstuck. You can begin right now. You can begin to declare the *101 Personal Forecast Confessions* at the end of this book—to begin your own comeback story.

With simple but powerful truths from God's Word and the resurrection power of Christ—you'll break free to make the difficult changes you long to make.

✱✱✱✱✱✱✱✱✱✱

The Most Powerful Scriptures
are the ones that you apply
to specific areas of your life.

Are you serious about getting victory
in every area of your life?

Establish a daily plan, on purpose,
of confessing and acting upon
specific Truths from the Word of God.

Become skillful in following the example
of our Lord Jesus.

Jesus spoke the words of the Father God
everywhere He went
and in every situation He encountered.

✱✱✱✱✱✱✱✱✱✱

"I am ready to perform My Word"
Jeremiah 1:12

✱✱✱✱✱✱✱✱✱✱

PERSONAL FORECAST STRATEGY 2

Take It By Force!
(Overcome the Past with Strong Faith)

"Grit your teeth," "bite the bullet," "take the hit," "fight the good fight of faith," "whatever it takes," "just do it!"

These are familiar sayings that many people have used to inspire themselves to overcome disappointments, setbacks, failures, and addictions.

Many people use their "pumped-up" inner human strength to prove that they can overcome life's challenges. We see it in the world of sports all the time. We call it a great comeback when the "underdog" rises to the occasion with the perfect combination of the adrenalin rush, pure guts, and athletic ability. With an abundance of energy and discipline—we can accomplish great things! *(We were created that way.)*

But this personal "thrill of victory" is just for a moment. For lasting victory, we need to surrender our incomplete, "finite" abilities and humble ourselves to our Heavenly Father—and rely on His perfect, *infinite* strength and power. We need strong faith in God and His Word to build a comeback testimony of the abundant life in Christ Jesus—that will inspire others to make a life changing come back through Christ.

The truth is that our greatest comeback victories happen on the inside first—in our faith-filled "spiritman." Others get to see the result afterward.

Strong In The Lord

"Finally, my brethren, be strong in the Lord, and in the power of His might"

Ephesians 6:10

It isn't a matter of becoming very smart or very strong physically. Many people have it all wrong. They have been looking around—seeing strong, smart people—and thinking: *"I'm just not smart enough—I just don't have that kind of faith."*

The truth is that we must become strong on the "inside." We have to get a revelation of being "Spirit-filled!" We need to understand that God has given us His Spirit to empower us to overcome in life!

Can you understand what that means? On the "inside" we are new creations; more than conquerors—and no weapon formed against us can prosper. Even when it "looks" like you have failed, when it looks like you have been defeated by your spiritual enemy—you can make a comeback!

That's why we can boldly say, *"I can do all things through Christ who strengthens me"* (Philippians 4:13).

Great "Comeback" Testimonies

I enjoy listening to personal testimonies about how people have developed a genuine personal fellowship with the Lord our God. I am inspired, energized, and challenged whenever I hear a story from someone who has discovered how much God cares—and how He is always ready to send them help from Heaven.

I've heard very dramatic stories of people who were addicted to drugs and alcohol—and all-of-a-sudden made a *radical "break free"* decision to follow the Lord Jesus.

I've witnessed overcoming stories of people who have endured hardships, some who have overcome sorrows, and some who have been healed after being sick, abused, broken-hearted, and in severe bondage to fear and anxiety.

It's Comeback Time!

It seems like it's becoming more common these days that people have phobias of all kinds that must be overcome. One person I know was afraid to leave the house—until the power of Christ and His Word became far more real than the fear!

Recently, I heard a man's story of being addicted to food—lots of it! He grew to a weight of 600 pounds, and was basically incapacitated. He finally realized the power of speaking and praying God's Word, and within 4 years he lost almost 400 pounds!

Another recent story of a famous "superstar" baseball player, who fell into a deep addiction to drugs and a hopeless depression, lost his professional baseball career and all of his possessions. Then, at his lowest point and looking like a complete failure—he got a hold of the some powerful Bible promises and asked the Lord to baptize him with the Holy Spirit and power. Now he has made a miraculous comeback to become one of the premier homerun hitters of the 21st century!

I also know a minister who had an extra-ordinary "overcoming story" of being set free from a life of being extremely religious. He had never cursed, tasted alcohol or cigarettes—and read Bible devotions every day of his life since the age of eight! This minister's comeback story eventually led him to an extremely thankful life of "knowing" the Lord as a child of the King, instead of just following religious *"do's and don'ts."*

God's plan is to reach out to "anyone who believes" with unshakeable, supernatural help from heaven.

Let Your *"Spiritman"* Rule!

Your spirit (heart) should rule in your life—not just *coping* or *managing*—ruling! (Your born again spirit should *rule* your soul and body.)

The apostle Paul presented this truth about how God created us—spirit, soul, and body all through the New Testament.

Most people spend their lives trying to satisfy their physical and emotional needs, like good food, clothes, money, houses, cars, etc. Many times when these needs are being fulfilled we are actually being controlled by our natural, physical man, instead of our "spiritman." *(The word "man" as used throughout the New Testament, refers to both man and woman, (as with the word "tiger").* In the lives of too many Christians their body and their emotions are "bossing" them around.

The "good fight of faith" must be won with spiritual weapons. Our victory is won in the spiritual world first—then it shows up in the physical world.

Some Christians *give up the fight* when they are flooded by negative emotions.

But not us!

We *pray* the powerful Word of God regardless of how we feel!

"We walk by faith, not by sight" (2 Corinthians 5:7).

As long as we are in this world, we are to fight the good fight of faith. And just like well trained marines, we should get our faith built up to the point where we follow orders, without question. There's where real victory is.

Are you battling with depressing thoughts, loneliness, or fear of getting sick? Then begin to follow orders. The orders that we have are to meditate day and night on God's eternal promises. And if we do, the blessing of God will be present in our lives. We were created that way!

We are "called out"—to be different. So there are issues to be decided. Do we want to be complainers or conquerors—wimps or warriors—pitiful or powerful—thankful or unbelieving?

Don't Be A Meat Head

Don't let the enemy knock you off God's best path. It's usually not the big things that get you off course—it's the small things. Over time they add up.

In these troubled times, we need to be far more *"spiritually minded."*

Every one of us ought to have a sincere desire to purify ourselves and to serve God wholeheartedly in every area of our lives—especially in the area of what we think about. Our attitudes and thoughts should be constantly changing for the better!

So my challenge to you today, is to make controlling your thought life a number one priority.

We can win the battle of the mind!

Reject Things that Are "Passed Away"

Many people make resolutions and set goals at the beginning of a new year. But after a few weeks have passed, many of them find they have failed to really change. I've got some good news for you today — it's not too late for you to make this the best year you have ever known!

The key to changing old habits for new ones and replacing failure with success lies in what we leave behind. In Hebrews 12:1 we read: "let us lay aside every weight, and the sin which doth so easily beset us, and let us run with patience the race that is set before us."

There are things that will limit your success, your victory and your joy — and I want to tell you how to lay them aside and *leave them behind* so that you can run the race God has planned for you.

Before you can leave those things behind, you need to stop and meditate on this truth — God has plans for your life. He wants you to know joy. He wants you to experience victory. He wants you to live in peace. He wants to fill your cup with blessings that overflow. That is what God has for you!

Here is the key truth — *you cannot take hold of the new until you let go of the old.* You cannot run the race looking back. You must learn how to let go of the past and reach toward the future.

Negative, fearful ways of thinking can cripple our faith and keep us from stepping into God's purpose and will for our lives. Leave them behind, and your future will be bright. If you do not, they will haunt, chase, hinder, oppress, terrorize and torment you.

Let It Go

Here are three things that you must leave behind to have the freedom to change your life for the better and enjoy God's very best.

First, we must lay aside all manner of unforgiveness. The devil wants you to be trapped by the things people did to you in the past. And when you do not forgive, he gets what he wants! In fact, when you harbor bitterness or anger over something that was done to you, you are opening a door for him to gain entrance to your heart.

He will capitalize on that to hinder and ruin your life. You are allowing him to manipulate and control your life when you do not forgive. You can't pick and choose whom to forgive—you have to forgive whoever has hurt you—even if, especially if, they don't deserve it.

In fact, it isn't forgiveness unless it really hurt first. If it didn't hurt, there's nothing to forgive.

The second thing we must leave behind is what I call "the disease to please." You cannot please God if you are living to please others. There are simply too many people with too many conflicting desires and dreams for you to please them all. This is true in every area of life.

The only ambition of your life should be to please God. Too many of us are slaves to what people think about us. We live our lives serving, not people, but our fear of what they think. Serving fear is a horrible way to live. It is filled with insecurity, doubt, dread, and ultimately failure.

If you live to please God, you will be free! You will still love people and give to them and serve them, but you won't be doing it to gain their attention and accolades. You will be doing it for the Lord.

Then finally we have to set aside guilt. Guilt is one of the most powerful forces the devil uses against us. If you let him, the enemy will beat you up with the sins and mistakes of the past. God wants you to live in freedom, not in guilt.

The blood of Jesus declares that you are not guilty!

Diligence and Willingness

God has a plan for our lives. It's up to each and every one of us to seek God's Will and to be sensitive to His silent voice. It's up to us to make sure that we don't allow the enemy to deceive us and get us off course to where we never reach the final destination that God has planned for each one of our lives.

Deuteronomy, chapter 28 talks about your diligence and willingness in listening to the voice of the Lord your God. If you obey His commands, multiple blessings will *overtake you*. In other words, if you can stay in the center of God's perfect will, you're going to have so many blessings come upon you that you can't even outrun them. I am thoroughly convinced about God's supernatural blessing for those of us that are diligent with His Word. I am thoroughly convinced that a supernatural peace and strength will overtake us if we simply make sure we're staying on God's best path for our lives—not going off to the left or right, but following the best path.

> *"Wherefore we also, since we are surrounded by so great a cloud of witnesses, let us lay aside every weight, and the sin which so easily ensnares us, and let us run with endurance the race that is set before us"*
>
> Hebrews 12:1

One version says, *"the particular race."* Another version says, *"Let us run steadily with determination, the course that is mapped out for our lives."*

This is an awesome thing to understand. If you can really grasp hold that the Creator of the universe, Almighty God, the One that spoke the world into existence, is so concerned about you. He loves you so much. You are so valuable to Him that He personally mapped out a specific course for your life.

But it's up to each one of us to make sure that we are sensitive to His voice and that we seek His ways

Seeking God's Guidance

God's best path for your life may not be the path that looks the most attractive. As strange as this may sound, God's best path may not be the job that pays the most money.

The enemy's specialty is to show you a path with an incredibly beautiful entry.

Now, think about this. A path may have luscious manicured flowers on each side. It may even have spectacular water fountains. You look carefully and you say, *Man, that's magnificent. Look at this path that God is leading me on. The pavement is paved so carefully.* But we've got to realize that sometimes that's a trick of the enemy.

Sometimes, the road begins to deteriorate into a narrow, bumpy, dirty, trashy road full of potholes, not to mention there's danger on each side. We might think, "*Man alive, what a deceptive entry that was. It looked so beautiful. If I'd known it was going to turn out like this, I'd never in a million years come down this road.*"

God can see the big picture. We are limited in our vision. We can only see so far. We can only see so much of the road.

Every one of us are going to face decisions and forks in the road. Maybe both ways have an equally beautiful entryway. It's up to us to seek God's will to know which one to take so that we don't get off course. God knows which road leads to danger. God can see it all.

Stay On Course

If we continually allow the enemy to deceive us and get us off course, we can literally waste half of our lives having to turn around and come back to the right road. We have to turn around and go all the way back just to return to the main course.

Sometimes we allow the enemy to steal valuable precious time from our lives. Time is one of the very few things that you cannot get back.

The enemy would love for us to waste our lives and not be everything God wants us to be. Even the people we associate with can get us off course.

"He who walks with wise men will be wise, But the companion of fools will be destroyed"

Proverbs 13:20

The trick of the enemy is to get us off course. He just tries to slowly and meticulously get us off course, so that we look up one day and we don't even realize it. We look up and think, *"My God in heaven, what happened to my life? I would have never dreamed I'd end up here, when I knew God wanted me over there.*

Then the enemy's next favorite lie is to tell you, *Well, there's no use in even going after the things of God. You've messed up so much you might as well just forget about it.*

Don't listen to that noise!

Stay Focused

I'm amazed at how many times I've wasted valuable time doing a thousand different things. (And they're all good.) They may even be in the name of the Lord. But the problem is that some of them were taking me away from what God was leading me to do.

Really, they're *weights* that are holding us back from receiving the true blessings that God wants to put on our lives. It's a favorite trick of the enemy—to get our minds so cluttered and so confused that we don't have any time to think about God. We don't have any time to meditate on Scriptures.

Another trick is to get your life so *busy* with so many extra-curricular activities that you don't have any time for God anymore.

We ought to make up our mind to run our race with extreme focus. You know, "Set your face as a flint" toward that goal.

Then I believe we'll be able to say like the apostle Paul, *"I have fought a good fight; I have finished my course—not somebody else's—I have finished my course and I have kept the faith."*

The Battle is Spiritual, Not Physical

Ephesians, Chapter 6, tells us that we are in a spiritual warfare. There's a battle going on all around us. It's taking place in the unseen spiritual world. You can even say it's going on in the mental realm too.

Your enemy has already been completely defeated. Jesus took care of him. The only power that he has is the power that he deceives you into *thinking* he has over you.

That's why the Bible talks about *"don't give any place to the enemy."* Don't give him any place in your mind. If you can learn to defeat the enemy in the area of your mind, you can win the battles of life. You can overcome in any situation.

Whatever you're going through or whatever comes against you in the future. You can learn to win!

You Are What You Think

Isn't it interesting that the enemy's favorite place to work is in our mind? Jesus called Satan in John 8:44 the "father of lies and all that is false."

The enemy can't touch your *spirit man*. But he can affect your thinking, your emotions, your personality, and your attitudes.

The only entrance that the enemy has into your life is through your mind.

Wow, what a powerful statement. Could that be true? That the only way the enemy can get to us is through our mind?

Immediately I think about stress that leads to physical sickness and disease.

Normally, when we think about winning the battle of the mind, we think about overcoming in areas like the emotional and mental areas—such as fear, worry, anxiety, and depression.

But here's another important question: Is it possible for us to allow Satan to bring sickness and disease into our lives by deceiving us in the area of our mind? Can we give the enemy a place in our mind and open up the door to where he can bring physical sickness and disease?

One Scripture comes to mind immediately—James 1:17. It says that, *"every good and perfect gift comes from the Father above."* God doesn't send sickness and disease to His children—that's the devil's handiwork. (See Acts 10:38 and John 10:10.)

Don't Open the Door

We would probably be very surprised at just how many times we "open the door" to the enemy and allow him to deceive us in the area of our minds. That's what gets us off track and out of God's perfect will.

We open up the door by our own actions to let the enemy bring mental anguish, mental torment, and even physical sickness and physical disease.

This is not meant to condemn you, but rather expose the way the deceiving enemy works. The Bible talks about *"knowing his strategies."* (Ephesians 6:11.)

If we are not diligent in the Word, we can get off track in our life and we move out of God's divine protection.

A Time to Pray and a Time to Resist

We've got to understand there's a time to pray and there's a time to stand strong and resist the enemy in the name of Jesus.

Many good Christian people don't understand that praying is not enough.

Don't get me wrong. Prayer is vitally important to the Lord and to the Christian life. But it's equally important to learn how to stand up on your own two feet—of your own will, boldly, forcefully, without any kind of insecurity, or fear, or inferiority—to resist the enemy in the name of Jesus. The Bible says if you do this, he'll go instantly. (See Matthew 18:18.)

Some of you might say, *If I do that, I'll stir the enemy up. He'll start to work overtime on me.*

If you think like that, the enemy will keep you in bondage. Hosea 4:6 says that people are destroyed for thinking like that. They're destroyed for a lack of knowledge. You've got to realize that God has already made a way for you.

Addiction Freedom

So many people live in bondage to addiction and habits. Sometimes this is a result of wrong thinking. They think that God doesn't love them—that God doesn't care about them—or that God is mad and not going to heal them.

If we would only realize that if we go one step toward God, we could know freedom like we have never known it before.

The *first* thing you've to got to do is to make Jesus the Lord of your life. You can't do it on your own.

The *second* thing you have to do is make a decision of your own will to get out of the situation you're in. You've got to make that decision. God will not go against your will. You have to do just like I did. You have to decide to do something about it.

And the *third* thing you've got to do is resist the enemy yourself and command him to get out of your life. And I promise you, you will walk free from those addictions.

****

My Personal Forecast Confession

In the name of Jesus my Lord,
I am now releasing my faith,
by confessing this to be the Lord's Day;
I will make it my best day In Christ!

I am what the Bible says I am.
I have what the Bible says I have.
I can do what the Bible says I can do.
I can do all things through Christ,
Who strengthens me.

I'm an overcomer
and more than a conqueror,
through Christ Jesus.

Thank You Lord!

****

"Let us hold fast our confession"
Hebrews 4:14

****

PERSONAL FORECAST STRATEGY 3

How To Walk On Water
(Aggressively Living by Faith)

Our high school football team was assembled in what we called the "upper room." It was right before a big game with our arch rivals across town. The *upper room* was a large balcony area above the basketball court. It had wall to wall cushioned mats for wrestling practice—and it was a great place sit down after being fully dressed with all our football pads and gear. It was the traditional place for the coach to give last minute instructions.

This time was a little different. The coach kept us waiting for an extra long time.

Finally, he came out with a half angry; half depressed look on his face—and it was obvious that he was carrying something behind his back.

What happened next was very unusual and surprising. He explained that he wasn't sure we should make the trip across town. He said he was seriously considering the possibility of cancelling this Friday night football game altogether.

Suddenly, our emotional coach jerked a rubber chicken from behind his back. He dramatically explained that he had just received this chicken by special delivery—with a note tied to its neck from the other team's coach. The note described in great detail that our team was a "bunch of cry baby losers!" It said that we were not even good enough to be on the same field with their grade school, "flag football" team.

To make a long story short—the coach accomplished his goal. We were stirred up and fighting mad. We drove on the bus across town in a full blown "football frenzy!"

We did things on the field that night that were far above all expectations. Our team won the game with some very unusual and surprising turn-over plays. We were so *pumped up*—we were so energized—we thought we could "walk on water!"

Your Power Moment

When you get your "break free" moment from discouragement, past abuses, sickness, fear, or addiction—you will feel like you are soaring with the eagles. If you can stir yourself up and start flowing with the supernatural power of the Holy Spirit—it will seem as though you can "walk on water!"

This spectacular phrase, "walk on water" is being used to emphasize that walking by faith and obedience to the Word of God is contrary to natural, "worldly" thinking. Instead of living your life in defeat—you can rise above the circumstances. You can follow the faith of Paul who proclaimed that through Christ He was *"more than a conqueror."*

One step of obedience in faith can change your life forever! You can demonstrate a great *"comeback" testimony* for Christ and His Word of promise. Today is your day to break free from every negative attitude of defeat—it's your day to turn around 180 degrees—it's your day to stop every ungodly habit, and go full steam ahead toward God's promises for your life.

At first these statements might seem to be a lot of hype, or just too good to be true. But I know from experience that the Spirit of the Lord will make "all things possible" for anyone who believes. (Mark 9:23.)

When God leads you to abruptly turn toward a new direction—even if it seems small and insignificant—that one step of obedience can thrust you into your destiny.

That's exactly what happened to us when God told us to start writing books about the power of a "personal forecast of God's Word." Just about the time that we thought our writing was strictly for our own spiritual growth—we began to have a strong leading to start a church. What could be a better name than *"Forecast For Life Church!"*

We had no idea the impact that one step of obedience would have on our destiny. We couldn't see how it was all going to work out.

We knew God told us to go ahead, but we did not know our entire future depended on it.

Our willingness, however, to follow that one instruction from God by faith changed our lives forever.

We've discovered that obedience—to God's Word and His Spirit—is the key to walking in the things God has planned for us. Obedience opens the door to destiny.

A Firm Foundation

God has given us His Word to instruct, convict, correct and train us so we won't get off course. That's what 2 Timothy 3:16 tells us. It says, *"All Scripture is given by inspiration of God, and is profitable for doctrine, for reproof, for correction, for instruction in righteousness."*

In order to walk in God's plan for our lives, we must know His Word. If we "do" the Word of God we'll prosper—if we don't, we won't.

God's Word teaches us how to live in obedience to God's will in thought, purpose and action. So, spending time in God's Word every day is important.

Matthew 6:33 tells us to *"Seek first the kingdom of God and His righteousness, and all these things shall be added to you."*

We seek first His kingdom and *His way of doing and being right* by knowing His Word. Then all other things are added unto us—the door to provision is opened.

Jesus also told us that. He said, *"If you abide in Me, and My words abide in you, you will[a] ask what you desire, and it shall be done for you"* (John 15:7). As we put God's Word in our hearts, our faith will grow. Then we can ask what we will—and it shall be done. *Abiding* isn't just reading the Word once in a while. It's meditating on the Word *continually.*

Living in a place of continual satisfaction and blessing is possible—all it takes is obedience to God's Word. When we give the

Lord our time and attention by putting the Word in front of our eyes, in our ears and our hearts, we can know His will and stay in it.

Look Forward — Move Forward

The truth is, God is not withholding vital information from us. He desires for us to know His will. Not only has He given us His written Word to keep us on course, He has "poured out" His Spirit to abide within us, empower us, and help us.

Psalm 143:10 is a wonderful prayer that talks about taking the right steps. It says, *"Teach me to do your will, for you are my God. May your gracious Spirit lead me forward on a firm footing"* (New Living Translation). We can count on the Holy Spirit to lead us forward on *firm footing*. He will teach us, lead us and direct us into God's plan. We don't have to stumble around in the dark trying to find our way.

In fact, God has already mapped out our course. He has planned a good life for us.

> *"For we are His workmanship, created in Christ Jesus for good works, which God prepared beforehand that we should walk in them."*
>
> Ephesians 2:10

Think about it! God has prepared paths for us to walk in. That, however, doesn't mean we don't have to do anything about it. We have the responsibility to take steps of obedience—whether little steps or big—by faith. We choose to walk in our destiny through steps of obedience.

If we head in a wrong direction, the Lord will let us know that too. The Holy Spirit will endeavor to get our attention and keep us on the right track. If we sense an uncomfortable scratching down in our spirits, that's Him letting us know we need to do or not do something.

For instance, you'll have that scratchy feeling if He is prompting you to break a negative habit. Or, if He is drawing you to spend more time in prayer, break free from a bad habit, or teach in "children's church," —you'll sense His leading or unction. Don't ignore that unction in your spirit—no matter what it is. Your destiny is waiting on the other side of your obedience!

If you need to make a change—make it. I realize at times you may not think you are able to do what the Holy Spirit is telling you to do, but if the Lord wants you to do it, you can! He has *equipped* you to walk in your destiny.

Hold Fast Your Confession

"Seeing then that we have a great High Priest who has passed through the heavens, Jesus the Son of God, let us hold fast our confession"

Hebrews 4:14

What are you confessing over your life today? The Bible says that life and death are in the power of the tongue. If you go around speaking doom and gloom, confessing that "Murphy's law" always happens to you, then that's exactly what you'll get. But when you allow the Word of God to direct your confessions, when you confess His blessing and promises over your life, it opens the door for God to move on your behalf.

That's why it's so important to "hold fast" to your confession of faith in Him. That means you can't go around confessing blessing one minute and doom and gloom the next.

That would be like trying to dig a hole by removing the dirt with one shovel full, and then putting it right back in with the next. You won't get anywhere!

In the same way, we have to hold fast our confession of faith in God and His goodness. Remember, He is a "rewarder" of those who diligently seek Him. As you diligently seek Him and hold fast your confession, you will rise up higher and see the victory and blessing the Lord has in store for you.

If you are serious about making a comeback in any area, pray this prayer:

Father in heaven, today I choose to speak words that glorify You. I choose to speak blessing over the people around me. Search my heart and remove anything that would keep me from honoring You with my words, thoughts, and actions.

In Jesus' Name. Amen.

Yeah But . . .

Some of you might be thinking, *"I don't talk to things or make a personal forecast about anything!"*

Don't be so sure about that. I've actually heard a man say, *"well, you know how it's going to be—I'll buy those new tires for my truck—and drive down the street and get a flat tire—Ha, Ha."*

That's his *forecast*! He was demonstrating God's creative power in words, and is doing what the Bible says about words: *"calls those things which do not exist as though they did." (Romans 4:17)*

When you develop a habit of talking that way—over time you will begin to believe it.

Just Do It Anyway!

Have you ever had a time in your life when you just couldn't get motivated? You knew what you wanted to do, you had the desire, but you just couldn't get motivated to take the first step.

When your get-up-and-go has gone and you find it difficult to get motivated to take action—consider this: You might be doing it wrong.

Experts in the field of human motivation tell us that instead of waiting until we are motivated to take action, we need to reverse the process and *take action to get motivated.*

Nothing makes us feel enthusiastic like *acting* enthusiastic. Nothing inspires creativity like getting started on a new project. Nothing gives us the energy to move ahead like taking that first step—and then another. Positive emotions and godly attitudes take their cues from your positive words of faith.

There are hurting people that need hear about your testimony and comeback victory. So, the next time you just don't feel like overcoming a challenge, just do it anyway!

Don't Tell It Like It Is

Words are serious business. As believers, we need to get serious about learning how to use them. We need to begin to put them to work for us like God Himself does. The Bible tells us that He uses words to "call those things which be not as though they were."

Most of us don't have the faintest idea how to do that. We've spent our lives "telling it like it is." We've consistently used our mouths to report on the "sorry state of affairs" around us. The very thought of calling "things which be not as though they were" seems a little crazy.

You might be thinking: *"You mean I'm supposed to say, 'I'm healed' when I'm feeling sick? I'm supposed to say, 'I'm prosperous' when I'm penniless?" "That sounds like lying to me."*

No. There's a vast difference between lying and speaking by faith. A lie is meant to deceive someone. It's designed to make someone believe something that's not true. But to speak by faith is simply to speak words that agree with the Word of God instead of the circumstances around you. It's speaking from your spirit instead of from your mind.

The Apostle Paul said it this way:

"And since we have the same spirit of faith, according to what is written,
'I believed and therefore I spoke.' We also believe and therefore speak"

2 Corinthians 4:13

There are some people who speak the words, but they don't have the faith to back it up. As a result, they fall flat on their spiritual faces. They didn't actually "call things that be not as though they were." They called things that be — the way they *wished* they were.

Those are two very different things. The words may be the same. But just wishing and hoping won't get the job done. You've got to "believe."

Begin today—bringing both your tongue and your heart in line with the Word. Stop telling it "like it is" and start speaking and believing the promises of God.

Your Spirit Can Believe

Each of us has been created to believe what we cannot see. We are a spirit, we have a soul—and we live in a body.

Our human intellect—our mind, will and emotions—cannot believe anything other than what we can already *see*.

Consequently, using our minds to try and believe for something we cannot see is like trying to plow a field with an ordinary pickup truck—instead of a tractor and plow. We can drive up and down the field all day, but we will never produce a crop.

While our minds were given to us to make decisions, our spirits were given to us to live by faith. Our spirits are where faith abides, where the love of God is, where hope lives.

The moment we decide to do something by faith, our *spiritman* should say, "*Hey, that's me—I can do that!*" We need to let our spirit take control of our emotions during the rush.

Finishing Touches on Faith

Jesus is the author, finisher, and developer of our faith.

That means, when we are determined to live by faith and pray God's Word—He is there to develop it, to stretch it, to cause it to grow. He does that by actively being the High Priest of our confession.

When we make the decision to live the life of faith and love—the next step is to begin practicing the Word of God.

Practicing the Word of God develops faith as we pray and declare specific Bible promises—and that's when you'll make a victorious comeback in every weak area of your life!

A Comeback From Inferiority

Have you ever been in the middle fighting one of life's storms only to realize that you are fighting more than one battle?

One storm is the one that is right "in your face," and the other is the baggage from the past you brought along with you. I'm referring to the bags of past hurts, insecurities, and fears.

Every negative emotion and reaction that we have is rooted with the inferiority that was passed down to us when Adam died spiritually. He became separated from the power of God, so he felt powerless—and as a result, inferior to what he was.

When we feel powerless that's when emotions dominate us and we tend to easily become angry, depressed, discouraged, vengeful, and susceptible to addictions. This is when we tear others down with gossip, or cutting remarks—in order to make ourselves feel more important and in control.

A Fresh Word Every Day

None of us can walk in the Spirit, or have strong faith without a fresh dose of God's Word every day. The truth is that many good Christians are just too weak in faith to "fight the good fight of faith."

Yesterday's meditating of God's Word is not good enough. It's "feeding" your *spiritman* meditating day and night, that brings victory over anything.

The Word of God is our Lifeblood! The Word is spiritual strength. The Word is life and peace.

It's really not that hard or painful. In fact, it's actually fun. It's like exercise—sometimes you don't "feel" like it, but when you "just do it" you are happy you did.

What will happen if you eat junk and don't work out? You get weaker and weaker—physically. Jesus said, *"man shall not live by bread alone, but by every Word that comes from God."* He also said that His Words were "spirit and life." If we just eat spiritual junk and don't *work out* our faith, we get weaker and weaker—spiritually.

Spirit Food

We all know we must prepare for physical competition with good food and exercise. But sometimes we are deceived into thinking we can do spiritual combat with a weak spirit. No way!

God's spiritual laws work just like the natural laws of gravity or electricity. They are working whether we believe it or not. We need to be aware that electricity will give you great blessing, or it will kill you! God's laws are given to us so that we can live an abundant life—and override evil and our spiritual enemy in the unseen world.

We need to be aware of the dangers of the unseen world and stay spiritually strong.

We only get strong in spirit and strong in faith by feeding on the Word of God. Then we exercise and release our faith by praying and confessing God's Word. It's just like I was taught about practicing "TaeKwonDo" blocks, kicks and punches—if you practice weak and pathetic, you'll do the same in a real test.

If our Word level is low, the devil can front-kick, side-kick, or spin-kick the tar out of you—defeating you with negative emotions and circumstances—because you allowed your faith to get weak.

You might think that this kind of Bible believing is a little too extreme. But in times like these—we need to be extreme! Extremely worry-free, extremely blessed, and extremely hopeful!

It's time we followed the example Jesus gave us from Matthew 4:4. He resisted the devil and his temptations by speaking God's Word. When the devil tempted him after he had not had food for 40 days—Jesus quoted Scripture: *"Man shall not live by bread alone, but by every word that proceeds from the mouth of God."*

It's Comeback Time!

****

"Breakfast of Champions" Prayer

Good morning, Heavenly Father;
You're my Refuge and my Fortress;
My Provider; my God; in You I will trust.

Good morning, Lord Jesus;
my Savior, Healer, Redeemer;
my Lord and King.

Good morning, Holy Spirit;
my Comforter, Helper, Strengthener,
and Teacher;

Please help me today in everything I do
and everything I say.

In Jesus' Mighty, Wonderful Name

****

*So shall My word be that goes forth
from My mouth;
It shall not return to Me void,
But it shall accomplish what I please,
And it shall prosper in the thing for which I sent it.*
Isaiah 55:11

****

PERSONAL FORECAST STRATEGY 4

Who's The Boss?
(A New Beginning – Let Your Spirit Rule)

"*You're not the boss of me!*" a little seven year old boy yelled.

It was right in the middle of his first day in our Children's Church auditorium. He was just like many other kids who were not raised in a good Bible believing church. He didn't know yet—but we were going to tell him the best news that he has ever heard in his very young life. We were not going to "boss him around"—we were going to teach him to say with confidence, *"God loves me—God cares about me!"*

I don't know if his home life was good or not so good. But over the next several weeks he became a brand new boy with a brand new attitude. This young boy learned to love coming to church every Sunday—learning to pray, and learning to boldly take authority in life with God's promises. He learned that sin and discouragement should not "boss us around."

We have authority in Jesus name, and our born again spirit is "boss" when it comes to overcoming sin, set-backs, past hurts, and the devil.

I remember another young boy about 10 years old came to our "Word Kid's Are Winners" Summer Camp with the same attitude. But this boy also had a very filthy mouth. What an awesome day it was when he surrendered his heart and life to the Lord! He experienced a dramatic *break free* transformation. He discovered that his new *spiritman* should be "boss" over his mind and body. *(Some parents don't even experience break free victories like these young ones!)*

The point is that God's Word of promise will work for anyone—no matter what your age—and no matter what you have experienced in the past. Your past and sin should not boss you around!

Your "Spiritman" Is boss

The Bible shows us that we are 3-part beings—spirit, soul, and body. Whenever we are addicted to something—(food, alcohol, TV, video games, worry, or negative thinking)—our body and soul is "bossing" us around. It should not be that way. Our faith-filled, Spirit-filled "spiritman" should be the boss! *(We were created that way!)*

This is the reason that most "rehab" programs do not make a permanent life-change. Most people—even good Christians—feed their bodies and souls *more* than their spirit. We need "faith food" every day: (God's Word: Romans 10:17; Matthew 4:4; John 6:63). Our spirit must be fed, and be stronger than our emotions, cravings, and desires.

Leave the Past Behind

Most of us know what it's like to suffer from failures, discouragement, and disappointments. But too few of us know what to do about them. So we limp along, hoping somehow the hurts and fears will just magically stop.

But it never happens that way. In fact, the passing of time often leaves us in worse condition—not better. Instead of putting those painful failures behind us, we often dwell on them until they become more real to us than the promises of God. We focus on them until we become bogged down in depression, frozen in our tracks by the fear that if we go on, we'll only fail again.

If depression has driven you into a spiritual nosedive, break out of it by getting your eyes off the past and onto your future—a future that's been guaranteed by Christ Jesus through the great and precious promises in His Word.

Forget about those failures in the past! That's what God has done (Heb. 8:12). If He doesn't remember them any more, why should you?

The Bible says God's mercies are new every morning. So if you'll take God at His Word, you can wake up every morning to a brand-new world. You can live life totally unhindered by the past.

So, do it! Replace thoughts of yesterday's mistakes with scriptural promises about your future. As you do that, hope will start taking the place of depression. The spiritual aches and pains that crippled you for so long will quickly disappear. Instead of looking behind you and saying, "I can't," look ahead and say, "I can do all things through Christ who strengthens me!"

The Greatest Comeback Of All Time

The secret that people have been searching for since time began—is the supernatural power to touch a bitter life and make it sweet.

Every human heart cries it out. Every person ever born longs for the power to turn sickness into health, loneliness into love, bondage into freedom and failure into victory. All mankind yearns to taste the full sweetness of abundant life.

But does such power really exist? Is there truly a secret that can make any life an abundant life?

Absolutely. If you've made Jesus Christ the Lord of your life, you've already tapped that secret. It's the secret of the Cross.

"What do you mean?" you might ask. *"The Cross is no secret. Lots of people know about the Cross."*

Lots of people may know some basic facts about the Cross, but most people don't understand the true power of it. If they did, then they'd know why the New Testament tells us quite plainly that *"the preaching of the cross is to them that perish foolishness; but unto us which are saved it is the power of God"* (1 Corinthians 1:18).

Notice that verse says the Cross *is* the power of God that brings us salvation (which means deliverance from all temporal and eternal evil) now, today, in the present—and every single day of our lives!

Everything good comes from the Cross. It changed the entire future of humanity and all of heaven forever.

The Cross affected everything. The problem is most of us don't even begin to understand the fullness of what happened there. We simply think of it as the place where Jesus paid the penalty for sin so that we could go to heaven and escape hell. That kind of thinking is right, as far as it goes. But it doesn't go far enough. There's much more to it.

Even the devil thought the cross was the "end." The devil thought the Son of God was down, out, and finished. But then Jesus was resurrected in power and glory—making it the greatest comeback of all time!

In the Beginning It Was All Good

To see just how much more actually happened at the Cross, we have to go back to the beginning, to the creation of man, to see how this all began. We have to go back and find out how bitterness got into the life stream of humanity in the first place. God certainly didn't put it there.

The book of Genesis tells us again and again that everything God created on the earth was good. He created the land and the water and "it was good" (Genesis 1:10). He created all vegetation and "it was good" (verse 12). He created the sun, moon and stars; He created the animals and every other living thing and saw that they were good (verse 25).

Once all that was done, God made the body of man from the dust of the earth and breathed life into him after saying, *"Let us make man in our image, after our likeness: and let them have dominion..."* (Genesis 1:26). At that moment, man became a living soul. He was clothed with God's own glory. God Himself empowered Adam (and later, his wife, Eve) to bring blessing and prosperity to the whole earth.

And when it was all finished, the Bible says that "God saw every thing that he had made, and, behold, it was very good" (verse 31). Those truly were the good old days.

The Touch of Death

Under the curse of sin, life on earth which had once been so sweet became indescribably bitter. In fact, "bitterness" is the *root* definition of the Hebrew word, "curse."

Before the curse of sin, Adam and Eve were free to enjoy God's good creation and reign in Eden as His representatives in the earth. They were free to enjoy nothing but sweetness and light forever—on one condition: They were to keep God's command.

Everything depended on that. If they obeyed God's command, life would be glorious and wonderful. If they disobeyed His command, they would die.

Sadly, they made the wrong choice. They disobeyed...and the light of God's glory that once radiated from them was snuffed out by the spiritual darkness of sin. Satan, whom they had obeyed, became their overlord. His deadly nature invaded their spirits, and everything beautiful God had breathed into Adam and Eve was instantly twisted and marred.

The fruit of God's Spirit that once filled their souls—qualities like love, joy, peace and faith—were suddenly corrupted. Love became hate. Joy became sorrow. Peace became turmoil. Faith became fear.

The Curse Hit the Earth

The anointing of God that had once empowered them to bless the earth was transformed into a touch of death that cursed the entire planet. The very ground itself was cursed because of what happened to them. Every molecule was infected by it. The earth, and everything in it, was cursed.

That, in itself, would have been bad enough. But the horror didn't stop there. Because God had ordained that every seed produce after its own kind, Adam and Eve were destined to reproduce children infected by the curse of sin. So the more they multiplied, the more the effects of the curse increased!

I doubt if Adam realized the full extent of what had happened right away, but as time passed the magnitude of it must have dawned on him. He must have thought, *Dear Lord, the seed of everything in the earth is bitter! My own seed is bitter! How will anything on earth ever be pure again? God, how can I ever be Your friend again?*

Adam didn't have a clue. He didn't know what God's plan was. It was a mystery hidden in God before the world began (1 Corinthians 2:7). Yet from the very first moment the curse hit the earth, God began to talk about redemption. Right there in the Garden of Eden after Adam sinned, God spoke to the devil and said, *There is One coming, the son of a woman, and He will crush your head....* (See Genesis 3:15.)

God Made A Way

The devil himself must have wondered how God was ever going to find such a man. After all, the entire race of man was under demonic lordship. They were all sinners. They couldn't defeat the devil. They were his slaves. And through their sin, they'd all earned the same wages: bitterness and eternal death.

According to God's system of covenant justice, if God could find one pure man, the blood of that man could be shed for the rest of mankind. He could become their substitute and take their punishment. But God had no pure seed on the earth to work with. He couldn't even start again from scratch to form a new Adam from the dust of the earth, because the dust itself was cursed and impure. How could God ever find human blood that was not already cursed with bitterness? It seemed impossible!

But God made a way. He visited a young woman named Mary and spoke His Word to her. She believed it and the Holy Spirit sent the Word into her.

> *"And the Word was made flesh, and dwelt among us, (and we beheld his glory, the glory as of the only begotten of the Father,) full of grace and truth"*
>
> John 1:14

Jesus, the Word Himself, was born as the pure, sinless Son of Man and Son of God. There was no bitterness in Him. No trace of the curse. He passed every test of temptation that Adam had failed. He lived as a free man. Death could not touch Him.

But then He did the unthinkable.

"And being found in fashion as a man, he humbled himself, and became obedient unto death, even the death of the cross"

Philippians 2:8

Jesus was already free. He didn't have to do that. But He chose to do it so *"...that through death he might destroy him that had the power of death, that is, the devil; and deliver them who through fear of death were all their lifetime subject to bondage"* (Hebrews 2:14-15).

Living in Heaven's Goodness

That's what happened on the Cross! Jesus redeemed us from the bondage of the curse by becoming a curse for us (Galatians 3:13). He not only paid the awful price for what Adam did, He broke the power of the curse and destroyed Satan's authority to use it on any believer who, by faith, will walk in their purchased redemption.

Jesus took away the authority of bitterness and released the blessing—heaven's goodness—back into the earth! He bore our bitterness and gave us His sweet abundant life.

He opened Eden's goodness to us again.

How do we live in that goodness? The same way Adam and Eve were supposed to do it—by obeying God's commandment. If we'll do that, the curse will be helpless to function in our lives and God's good blessings will overtake us (Deuteronomy 28:1-2). The saving power of the Cross itself is released in every area of our lives— spirit, soul and body—when we keep God's commands.

Believe and Love

And as 1 John 5:3 says, *"His commandments are not grievous."* In fact, they are surprisingly simple.

> *"This is his commandment, That we should believe on the name of his Son Jesus Christ, and love one another"*
> 1 John 3:23

Or, as Jesus said in Matthew 22:37-40: *"'You shall love the LORD your God with all your heart, with all your soul, and with all your mind.' This is the first and great commandment. And the second is like it: 'You shall love your neighbor as yourself.' On these two commandments hang all the Law and the Prophets."*

Believe and love. That's all we have to do to live free.

There's no need for us to suffer the effects of the curse any longer. Through Jesus' death and resurrection, God has not only made it possible for us to taste the sweet life of God, He's put a well of it inside us (John 4:14). He's given us rivers of it, rivers that will never run dry (John 7:38).

The supernatural power to touch a bitter life and make it sweet has already been given to you. So release your faith and let that sweetness flood not only your own life, but the lives of countless others as well. Step into a sweet "comeback" through the power of the Cross!

Only You Can Prevent the Fire

> *"The tongue is a little member, and boasts great things. Behold, how great a matter a little fire kindles! And the tongue is a fire, a world of iniquity: so is the tongue among our members, that it defiles the whole body, and sets on fire the course of nature; and it is set on fire of hell"*
> James 3:5-6

Your "spiritman" is the boss—and the boss should rule with "Words." Use them right and they'll move mountains. Use them wrong and they can cause your entire life to go up in smoke.

You may say, *"I find it hard to believe that major catastrophes can be caused by a few simple words. I just can't see the connection."*

Look again at the phrase James used. "How great a matter a little fire kindles!" Have you ever lit a few little pieces of kindling wood and set them in the fireplace beneath a stack of logs?

What happened?

Most likely, the fire began to spread first to one log then to another until finally you had a great big blaze going. After it was over, you couldn't go digging around in the ashes to find the kindling that started it all, could you? No! It would be burned. There would be no trace of it at all.

The tongue is like that. It first defiles the body, then sets on fire the whole course of nature with a blaze so great that it leaves no natural trace of its origin. The words that started it end up so deeply buried in the ashes that you would never even know they were there.

So, don't ever underestimate the power of your words. I can assure you, Satan doesn't. He works constantly to get you to turn them in a negative direction. He'll fire darts of pain and sickness and discouragement at you just to get you to speak faithless words—words that will eventually send your life up in smoke.

Don't let him succeed. Instead, put out that fire by following the instructions in Ephesians 6:16. Do as the Apostle Paul says and "above all, taking the shield of faith, wherewith ye shall be able to quench all the fiery darts of the wicked."

Speak words of faith and stop the fire before it starts today!

Overcoming Challenges

In many of the challenges I have faced, something would happen as I listened to a Bible tape or attended a church service. The Word of God would correct me, drive out the disobedience or unbelief and destroy what was holding me down. Hearing the Word would bring me out of discouragement. It would stir up my faith again. I would start believing and saying that I had the victory in Christ.

Although nothing in the natural changed immediately, something happened in the supernatural. Something happened in my heart. God saw it too—He looks at our hearts. He hears our words. He knew faith was there. The turnaround came! The mountain was moved!

It pays to speak words that please God.

So, if wrong words come out of your mouth, repent and get back on the truth of the Word. When you speak words that are opposed to what you're believing for, repent and say, *"I break the power of that in the Name of Jesus. I'm believing the Word of God, and I'll not accept that opposing word coming out my mouth. Father, forgive me."*

Make all your words agree with the Word of God. Speak faith words that give your heavenly Father the freedom to do what pleases Him most—to bless you with the abundance of His life and provision.

Give God the pleasure of entering your words of faith in His book of remembrance. Let Him note you are one of those who believe Him and speak about His goodness.

Moving Mountains

As a born-again believer, you have residing within your spirit the faith of God. Faith is a fruit of the reborn human spirit (Galatians 5:22).

Faith must be in the unseen before it can be applied to the things you can see. It is cultivated through fellowship with the Father.

Your relationship with the Father God is the most important aspect of your faith walk. You cannot see God, but He will reveal Himself to you through His Word, by the Holy Spirit.

Faith that moves mountains is simply trusting God to keep His Word. You cannot trust God without knowing Him. Fellowship with God, Who is invisible, energizes the kind of faith that can change things in the visible, physical realm. It is quality time in prayer and study with the Father God. It will develop your trust and confidence in Him—and will enhance your faith because you are giving Him the opportunity to reveal His extraordinary love and strength to you. You will "know" Him.

You can also promote the development of your faith through your *personal forecast* of the Word of God. Faith is an action; when you believe that you receive, you will act like it—you will forecast it for your life.

God told the prophet Joshua, *"This Book of the Law shall not depart from your mouth, but you shall meditate in it day and night, that you may observe to do according to all that is written in it. For then you will make your way prosperous, and then you will have good success."* (Joshua 1:8.)

Bible Meditation

Meditation reveals how to act on the Word. Confession or forecasting is part of meditation. When you are speaking the Word to yourself, you are meditating the Word. You cannot say one thing and think something else. What you meditate regulates what you believe. Meditation and confession will enable you to believe God's Word enough to act on it in faith.

Faith is also developed through praying in the spirit. Jude 20 says, "But you, beloved, building up yourselves on your most holy faith, praying in the Holy Spirit." As you spend time every day, praying in the Holy Spirit, you are keeping your spirit active rather than passive. You will be built up and made stronger in faith.

Guard Your Thoughts

The Bible is very clear about the importance of guarding your mind and controlling your thought life. Your mind plays a vitally important role in your walk of faith. When you made Jesus the Lord of your life, the Holy Spirit infuses the life of God into your spirit, and you were changed. The Bible says, we become new creatures in Christ Jesus.

But it is so important for us to understand that although God makes our spirit completely brand new, he doesn't do anything to our physical bodies or to our minds. He leaves both of those areas up to us to take care of. Satan's favorite area to work in is in the area of your mind. He cannot touch your Spirit man once you're born again.

The Bible says, you're in the palm of God's hand and no man can snatch you away. But the enemy can deceive you in the mental area if you allow him to. Jesus called Satan in John 8:44, the father of lies and all that is false. And I can't think of any area that keeps more people in bondage than this area of our thought life. Satan specializes in worry, fear, anxiety, confusion, and doubt. He is a master deceiver and he knows that he can control and manipulate our whole lives by simply affecting the way we think.

Block the Doorway

Your mind is Satan's target. The only entrance Satan has into your personality, your emotions, into your thoughts is through your mind. But fortunately, you control that ever important doorway. The only access the enemy has in your life is the access you allow him to have. That's why the Bible tells us not to give *"place to the devil."* (Ephesians 4:27.)

Don't give him any place in your mind or in your thoughts. You've got to be very selective and very cautious about what you choose to think about. You've got to take control of your life by standing guard over your thought life.

The Bible says in Proverbs 23:7: *"For as he thinks in his heart, so is he."* You will eventually become what you think. You can't think one thing and become something else. If you allow yourself to think negative worried, fearful thoughts—then you will become a negative, worried, fearful person. You cannot think defeat and expect victory. You can't think poverty, and expect wealth. You can't think the worst, and expect the best.

You've got to consider and *weigh* what you're thinking about. Take regular inventory of your thought life. You've got to be extremely careful and extremely aware about what you allow your mind to think about. And what you choose to dwell on. Satan would love to keep you living a life of defeat by causing you to think thoughts of worry and anxiety and fear. He knows if he can keep our minds all cluttered and confused, we will never be the person God wants us to be.

Resist the Negative Flow

God gives us a phenomenal promise for peace in every situation. It's very simple. Yet it's really profound—it's powerful! The Bible says, *"You will keep him in perfect peace, Whose mind is stayed on*

You, Because he trusts in You. Trust in the Lord forever" (Isaiah 26:3-4).

Notice there is something that we all have to do if we're going to experience perfect peace. We've got to control our thought life. We've got to guard our minds. We've got to think on the things of God. But this is not going to happen automatically. This has got to be a decision you continually make throughout life.

We live in a very negative society. This culture focuses on what's wrong and not what's right—what's missing, instead of what we have right now—what's ugly, not what's beautiful. Pick up a newspaper today or watch the News tonight and see if the major focus isn't on the negative. Every one of us are going to have plenty of opportunities to dwell on the wrong things. The enemy is constantly bombarding our minds with ungodly negative thoughts that are trying to confuse us and distract our attention away from the things of God.

The enemy is doing his best to slowly and very cunningly infiltrate your mind and bring thoughts of fear and uncertainty about the future. Satan specializes in fear. Fear of not having our needs met. Fear of not being accepted. Fear of failure. Fear of being stuck in the affects of tragedy. Fear of not living a healthy life. This fear creates anxiety, worry, doubt, unbelief, and confusion.

But we can resist this negative flow of fear with the name of Jesus and the Word of God!

Faith Vs. Fear

Fear is a force just like faith is a force. If you give in to fear and start to dwell on that junk and start to act on it, that fear can actually bring things to pass just like faith can bring things to pass. Job said, "the thing I greatly feared came upon me."

You and I choose every single day what we're going to think about, whether good or bad. And if we let ourselves, we can all think of a thousand negative things that might happen to us. What if my business goes down? What if I have an accident? What if my child gets on drugs? What if? You can worry yourself silly if you want to.

Some of you think, *You know, that's just the way I am. Mom and Dad used to worry. Grandma and Grandpa used to worry. They were all negative people. Our whole family always worries. We're professional worriers. That's just the way God made me.*

No, that is not true. Worrying is a choice. You should rise up today in the name of Jesus and just break that habit. Refuse to listen to Satan's lies. You've got to refuse to let your mind dwell on that junk.

The Bible tells us what we should dwell on in Philippians 4:8. It's to *"think on things that are pure and honest and of a good report."* Things that build you up, not tear you down.

Think on all the great things God has done for you. In other words, you should dwell on the positive and not the negative. Quit thinking about what you *don't* have and start thinking about what you *do* have. Quit thinking about what's *wrong* with you and start thinking about what's *right* with you.

Quit thinking about how big your problem is and start dwelling on the fact of how big your God is.

No Worries!

We've got to learn to live a grateful life and always focus on the positive—not the negative. If you're continually thinking about the goodness of God, you're not going to have any time to worry and complain and get down and discouraged. If you're always meditating on God's promises, then you're always going to be filled with a good report.

The words that come out of your mouth are going to be faith-filled words. You're going to be solid and consistent because it's not going to matter what your circumstances are. It only matters what God's Word says.

In life, situations and circumstances are constantly changing. But thank God the good news is that we serve a God that never changes. He is consistently good. He is there all the time. He'll never leave us nor forsake us. He's the solid rock.

The promises in God's Word will never pass away.

Conquering the Spirit of Fear

You were not given the spirit of fear (2 Timothy 1:6-7). You were given the gift of love, which casts out all fear. You must stir up the gift inside of you.

When you walk in the love of God, you walk in His power. Fear is the spirit of Satan.

Satan used fear to trick Eve in the Garden of Eden (Genesis 3:1-6). Eve feared that God was withholding something from them.

Immediately after they sinned, Adam and his wife became fearful.

The root of all fear is in the belief that God's Word won't come to pass. Many people don't believe that God will supply their needs (Philippians 4:19), or that by His stripes they are healed (1 Peter 2:24). You must make a decision to believe the Word of God.

Do not be deceived into believing that fear is a good motivator. There is torment in fear. Satan is motivated by fear. God is motivated by faith.

The fearful and the unbeliever arrive at the same destructive end (Revelation 21:8).

Unbelief is made wicked because of the presence of fear.

Job's fear connected his household to destruction (Job 1:1; 3:25).

Fear and faith operate by the same principles and are both spiritual connectors. Faith comes by hearing God's Word. Fear comes by hearing Satan's words.

In these last days men's hearts will fail because of fear (Luke 21:26)

Faith Can Be Seen

Your faith is reflected in the things you do. You can tell when a person has faith by the way they walk, talk and carry themselves; their faith is evidenced by their actions.

Faith is an attitude that must be displayed through your action.

Corresponding action is action that agrees with, fits or reflects your faith. For example, if you are believing God for the money to pay a bill, an example of a corresponding action would be to write a check in the amount you are believing for and keep it in your drawer until the money manifests.

Perform actions that harmonize with your current faith level. Acting beyond your current faith level causes problems. For example, writing bad checks and believing God for the money to show up before the check clears is not faith; it is illegal.

Sometimes corresponding action is simply resting in the confidence that God has already taken care of your situation. Faith without proper corresponding action is ineffective (James 2:17-18).

The Word of God must be combined with faith in order to yield results (Hebrews 4:1-2). When you have confidence in God's ability to bring His Word to pass, you will be willing to go to extreme lengths to demonstrate your faith. For example: The men in Mark 2:1-5 tore the roof off a house to get a sick man to Jesus so he could be healed.

Doing whatever God tells you to do guarantees results (John 1:1-11).

When God tells you to do something and you do it, you are acting in faith.

In John 1:1-11, the water was turned into wine because the servants acted on what Jesus told them to do; their corresponding action activated their faith and a miracle took place.

Noah started building an ark when he received a warning from the Lord about future events. His confidence in what God said prompted him to act out on what he heard and activated his faith (Hebrews 11:4).

****

Forecast Confession for Blessing

Today I let the Word of Christ
dwell in me richly.
I will meditate and obey
the Word of the Lord my God.

Therefore, I believe and receive
wisdom, blessing and favor
everywhere Your Spirit leads me to go.

I'm so thankful Lord,
that my blessing and favor
will be for Your glory,
for my benefit,
and to bless everyone I meet.

In Jesus' mighty Name!

****

*"Hold fast the confession of our hope
without wavering,
for He who promised is faithful."*
Hebrews 10:23

****

PERSONAL FORECAST STRATEGY 5

Activate the Power of the Holy Spirit
(Surrender Your Will to God's Ways)

I pray and sing "in the spirit" every day. I surrender my own will to the leading and teaching of the Holy Spirit—and begin to privately pray with a wonderful heavenly, unknown tongue.

Does that Surprise you?

No matter where we are on planet earth, we can enter the "secret place" of prayer to the Most High God—in the wonderful name of Jesus—where the Holy Spirit gives powerful holy sounds, syllables, and spiritual words. It's the true worship *"in the spirit."*—that our Lord Jesus taught about. (See John 4:23-24 and 1 Corinthians 14:14.)

It's the same phrase used by the apostles Paul and John. It's a private, supernatural prayer to the Heavenly Father, through the Holy Spirit, in Jesus' mighty, holy name.

Humbling ourselves "in the spirit" of the Lord is one the most awesome things we can experience on planet earth!

Have We Resisted the Wrong Thing?

Don't misunderstand. At first I did not want this to happen to me. I was just like a lot of other Christians that are discouraged (by well-meaning church leaders) from receiving something thought to be un-natural and not normal.

When I heard the good news that the Holy Spirit is alive and well on planet earth, I was amazed and very hungry to find out more! You see living a normal, natural life is really just conforming to what society, organized religion, and the 6 O'clock News tells us.

Shouldn't we be living by what Heaven tells us?

It's sad to see that many well-meaning Christians are living the "same ole, same ole" life—waking up to another day of going to work, coming home, and watching TV—then praying for the weekend, to get some temporary desires satisfied.

What if life could be an exciting adventure every day?

What if we could live life in a super-natural way—doing the works of Jesus and helping people with words and healing from heaven?

We can! We can soar much higher than our physical senses can take us. *(Jesus promised that we could.)*

It's Better If I Go Away

The disciples of Jesus were "eye-witnesses" to the most phenomenal and glorious miracles the world has ever seen!

The disciples were amazed as blind eyes were opened and the dead were raised to life. The disciples heard Jesus command a raging storm to die and a fig tree to wither. They saw thousands fed as Jesus multiplied a few fish and loaves of bread. The words of many prophets of God were coming to pass right before their very eyes!

Never before had mankind witnessed the miraculous hand of God in such an overwhelming and personal way.

Yet, as wonderful as things seemed to be—the disciples were told by Jesus Himself that it would be better if He went away. He said that the Heavenly Father had a far more excellent plan for them—and it would be to their "advantage" if He returned to heaven. (See John 16.)

The Holy Spirit Is Waiting On You

You are not an accident. God has a divine plan for your life, and this great plan will be fulfilled as you are led by the power of the Holy Spirit!

The number one thing you and I need to know is that God cares about you. He loves you!

For I know the thoughts that I think toward you, says the LORD, thoughts of peace and not of evil, to give you a future and a hope. Then you will call upon Me and go and pray to Me, and I will listen to you. And you will seek Me and find Me, when you search for Me with all your heart.
Jeremiah 29:11-13

The second thing that we should all realize is that *"God is on our side,"* we do not have to fear the unseen, supernatural world if we trust our Creator. (See Psalm 118:6.)

The "Unseen" World Is Real

If we are going to trust in the Lord for a blessed life, then one vital fact should be settled in our thinking: The "unseen" world is more real than the seen world—and this supernatural world has a dramatic effect on everything that happens in the "seen" world.

In the unseen world there are angelic spirits and demonic spirits, there is a real heaven and a real hell—and of course there is the unseen Lord God Himself, Creator and Sustainer of everything!

Another thing to remember when you are praying to receive the "secret power of God, the Holy Spirit," is that He is a gentleman and will never force you—but always waits until you open your heart to choose Him.

Your spirit—your heart—the "hidden man of the heart" the eternal you on the inside—has been made in the image of God.

You might be thinking: *"That doesn't sound like what I have heard in my church."*

You're right! Usually the only time we hear anything about the unseen world is at funerals. Do you want to wait until your funeral to find out if there is really an invisible world?

The Bible definition of faith is that it is the substance and evidence of things that cannot be seen.

"Everyone" Has Faith In The Unseen

Everyone has faith and everyone believes . . . something.

What about your actions when the weather predictions are indicating a major storm might be heading your way? You look outside and it's a clear day, yet you start making plans to take cover, relocate, or board everything up. By faith you start acting based on what you have been told.

Most of our every day activities are done by faith.

Do you wake up every morning and head toward your car by faith, believing that it will start and get you to work? It is something that you cannot see while you are in the shower, but your evidence is that the mechanic said the vehicle is all tuned up and ready to go.

What do you do when your boss tells you that a firing is about to take place if you do not get to work? By faith you believe it and get back to work. Your evidence? The person that used to sit next to you until last week is not there anymore.

You can't see the air you breathe (I'm not talking about polluted air). But there is "unseen" evidence that air is flowing through your lungs and you are alive!

You can't see atomic or hydrogen molecules, but we believe that our world is in danger everyday because of "nuclear" weapons. The evidence? We have been given detailed physical evidence by reputable news reporters, scientists, and historians.

Human beings were created to live by faith.

For since the creation of the world His invisible attributes are clearly seen, being understood by the things that are made, even His eternal power and Godhead, so that they are without excuse.

Romans 1:20

Help From Heaven

It is imperative that we get an understanding that there is an unseen world all around us.

If you are searching for the safest way to live in this violent world, and are not satisfied with typical religious thinking, you have to know how to get help from Heaven.

Satan is alive and well on planet earth. He makes himself visible by every evil manifestation that you can see. Look around.

The works of the devil are obvious in every corner of the world, in every news broadcast, in every mental institution, in every devil worshipping cult, and in every poverty stricken 3rd world country. However, I do not want to give "the salesman of fear" any more press. What we need is to magnify the goodness of Almighty God. God is love, He offers hope, supernatural protection, and gives real peace to overcome the evil of this *seen* and *unseen* world.

In light of the many examples in God's Word (Jesus, Noah, Abraham, David, Daniel, Shadrack, Joshua, Moses, Elijah, Peter, and Paul), we can expect supernatural protection. God's promises belong to us. It's not because of anything we have done. It's entirely because of what Jesus has done.

Are there conditions to God's protection? Absolutely.

Have we fulfilled all of the conditions? Not by a long shot.

We have a long way to go in order to get ourselves to believe what God has promised. But we can get there!

Believe Before You See

Remember the Lord's Prayer? *"Thy will be done on earth as it is in Heaven."* Jesus was calling for God's will, from the unseen heaven, to be done in the earth. In the book of James we are taught that, *"every good and perfect gift comes down from the Father of Lights,"* (James 1:17).

So, our prayers are calling for God's goodness in the "unseen" world of Heaven, to manifest in our "seen" world.

Having said that, we should also consider that human nature is to say; *"I'll believe it when I see it."*

But the truth is that we need to believe "first."

If there was ever a generation where people need to be aware of God's "unseen" world and know how things operate there, it's this generation.

You'll never understand the truth of God's Creation, His ways, His Word—unless you "submit" your own will and ways to God's Will and ways.

It's A "Hidden" Secret

The most wonderful promises of God are reserved especially for "you" – the born again, Spirit-filled believer!

> *"Attaining to all riches of the full assurance of understanding, to the knowledge of the mystery of God, both of the Father and of Christ, In whom are hidden all the treasures of wisdom and knowledge,"*
> Colossians 2:2b-3

It is the "unsearchable riches of Christ that "unbelievers" cannot understand. Our preaching of the Good News is to *"make all see what is the fellowship of the mystery, which from the beginning of the ages has been hidden in God who created all things through Jesus Christ,"* (Ephesians 3:9).

The wonderful mysteries of the goodness of God are hidden from the devil, enemies of the cross, and anyone who practices evil.

> *"But we speak the wisdom of God in a mystery, the hidden wisdom which God ordained before the ages for our glory. Which none of the rulers of this age knew; for had they known, they would not have crucified the Lord of glory"*
> 1 Corinthians 2:7-8

> *But as it is written:*
> *"Eye has not seen, nor ear heard, Nor have entered into the heart of man the things which God has prepared for those who love Him."*
> *"But God has revealed them to us through His Spirit. For the Spirit searches all things, yes, the deep things of God"*
> 1 Corinthians 2:9-10

God's Will Is the Baptism With the Holy Spirit

You have been involved with the Holy Spirit since you first accepted Jesus as your Lord and Savior.

When you prayed a sincere prayer according to Romans 10:9 and confessed that Jesus was raised from the dead to give you salvation—it was the Holy Spirit who performed the miracle of the "new birth" of your spirit.

1st Corinthians 12:3 states that no one says "Jesus is Lord" except by the Holy Spirit.

Jesus Himself told the men who walked by His side for 3 years that it is to their "advantage" if He went away and sent them the Holy Spirit.

Just think of that!

Would you like the inside information that will guide you through the bad news and uncertainties of this world?

All you have to do is ask the Father in Jesus' name to be filled with the Holy Spirit. Your only job is to believe and receive—and Jesus has promised to baptize you with the overflowing "rivers of living water" power of the Holy Spirit!

> *"So I say to you, ask, and it will be given to you; seek, and you will find; knock, and it will be opened to you. For everyone who asks receives, and he who seeks finds, and to him who knocks it will be opened. If a son asks for bread from any father among you, will he give him a stone? Or if he asks for a fish, will he give him a serpent instead of a fish? Or if he asks for an egg, will he offer him a scorpion? If you then, being evil, know how to give good gifts to your children, how much more will your heavenly Father give the Holy Spirit to those who ask Him!"*
>
> Luke 11:9-13

The Power of the Holy Spirit In You

Believers today have vastly underestimated the power of the Holy Spirit.

You may wonder how I can be so sure of that. It's simple, really. If we truly understood and believed what the Bible tells us about Him, we would never worry about anything again. All hell has to offer could come against us and we wouldn't fear. We'd just grin and say, "Bring it on, devil! The Greater One lives within me and He has given me all the wisdom, strength, power and provision I need to crush you like a bug."

Right now you may think you could never have that kind of boldness. But let me ask you something: What would you do if Jesus appeared to you today? How would you act if He linked His arm in yours and told you that from now on, He would be physically present with you in every situation? If you became sick, He would lay His hand on you and you'd be healed. If you ran short of money, He'd pray and multiply your resources. If you encountered a problem you didn't know how to handle, He'd tell you exactly what to do.

Under those circumstances, you'd be very bold and confident, wouldn't you? Every time you ran into trouble, you'd just glance over at Jesus standing next to you and suddenly, you'd have great courage.

Of course, there's one problem. The fact is, you don't have that advantage. You don't have Jesus standing next to you in the flesh taking care of your every need.

But you do have something *better*.

I realize it's difficult to believe there's anything more beneficial than Jesus' physical presence. But there is. Jesus said so Himself.

That's right. In the hours just before He was crucified, He told His disciples that He would be leaving them and returning to His Father in heaven. When they expressed their sorrow and dismay, He said:

> *"And I will pray the Father, and He will give you another Helper, that He may abide with you forever—the Spirit of truth, whom the world cannot receive, because it neither*

sees Him nor knows Him; but you know Him, for He dwells with you and will be in you. ....Nevertheless I tell you the truth. It is to your advantage that I go away; for if I do not go away, the Helper will not come to you; but if I depart, I will send Him to you."

John 14:16-17, 16:7

To fully grasp the impact of this last statement, you have to realize that Jesus was talking to a group of men who had followed Him day and night for three years. They had seen His miracles. They had enjoyed perfect protection and provision at His hand.

Peter was sitting there among them. Can't you just imagine what was running through his mind? No doubt he was thinking of the first time Jesus had borrowed his boat. After He'd finished preaching from it, He'd said to Peter, "Grab your nets and we'll go catch us some fish." It was the middle of the day. Peter knew you couldn't catch fish in the daylight in that lake—the water was too clear. The fish would see the net and run from it.

But just to humor Him, Peter had done what Jesus said and ended up with a net-busting, boat-sinking load of fish. What a day!

Then there was the time Jesus healed Peter's mother-in-law of a deadly fever. Cured her instantly!

Even that didn't hold a candle to what happened on the Mount of Transfiguration. That day Peter had actually seen Moses and Elijah talking with Jesus. He had watched His body transfigure before his very eyes. He'd seen the shining cloud of glory and heard the awesome voice of Almighty God!

As those events passed through Peter's mind, he must have wondered, *How can it possibly be expedient or to my "advantage" for Jesus to go away?*

Knowing that question was in the heart of every one of His disciples, Jesus said, in essence, *"I know this is hard for you to believe, but trust Me on this. I'm not lying to you. It's better for you if I go away so that I can send the Holy Spirit to not only be with you, but to be in you!"*

The Power of God

It's been more than 2,000 years since Jesus foretold the importance of the Holy Spirit—and most of us are still struggling to fully believe it.

Theologically, we know it's true, and we thank God that we're born again and baptized in the Holy Ghost. But then we open our mouths and say things like, "If I could just feel Jesus' hand on my forehead, it would be easier for me to receive my healing."

Why is that?

I believe it's because we haven't truly appreciated the might and the ministry of the Holy Spirit. We haven't yet had a full revelation of Who this is that is living inside us.

Many Christians, for example, seem to think the first time the Holy Spirit did much of anything was on the Day of Pentecost. But that's not true. The Holy Spirit has been at work on this planet ever since the beginning.

Look at the Book of Genesis and you can see that for yourself. There in the first few verses we find:

"In the beginning God created the heaven and the earth. And the earth was without form, and void; and darkness was upon the face of the deep. And the spirit of God moved upon the face of the waters. And God said, Let there be light: and there was light."

Genesis 1:1-3

Think about that! The Holy Spirit was hovering, waiting to supply the power to create. Then the moment God spoke the Word, *"Light be!"* (literal Hebrew translation), the Spirit sprang into action and supplied the power to bring this universe into being.

That's how the Bible introduces us to the Holy Spirit!

You see, the Holy Spirit is the power of God. Every time you see God's power in action, you can be sure the Holy Spirit is on the scene.

When the Holy Spirit came on Samson, he single-handedly killed a thousand Philistine soldiers (see Judges 15:14-16). Can you imagine how embarrassing that must have been for the Philistines who escaped?

Some people get the idea that Samson was able to do those great exploits because he was a giant of a man. But he was really just an ordinary fellow. He only became extraordinary when the Spirit of God came on him.

The prophet Elijah was the same way. On his own, he was just as normal as you and me. He was once so frightened by the threats of a woman that he hid in the wilderness and asked God to kill him so he wouldn't have to face her.

But when the Holy Spirit came on him, Elijah was a powerhouse. He once called down fire from heaven, killed 400 prophets of Baal, and outran the king's chariot (drawn, no doubt, by the fastest horses in the nation of Israel). And he did it all in one day (see 1 Kings 18-19).

The Most Amazing Mind!

Don't get the idea from those examples that the Holy Spirit is simply a mindless source of raw power. Far from it! When He moves in on a situation, He does it with wisdom and understanding so vast that it staggers the human mind.

Isaiah 40:13 says of Him: *"Who hath directed the spirit of the Lord, or being his counselor hath taught him?"* Now go back and read how verse 12 further explains: *"Who hath measured the waters in the hollow of his hand, and meted out heaven with the span, and comprehended the dust of the earth in a measure, and weighed the mountains in scales, and the hills in a balance?"*

Consider for a moment what kind of mind could take a handful of water, weigh it and then compute all the moisture changes of the earth that would take place over untold thousands of years.

What kind of mind could take a handful of dust, weigh it, and then figure out how to form the earth—mountains and all—in such a way that it would always stay in perfect balance?

That's the kind of mind the Spirit of God has!

When He put this earth together, He did it so perfectly that it can travel 1,000 miles an hour in one direction and 10,000 miles an hour in another, both at the same time, without ever getting the slightest degree off course. He constructed it so that it could compensate for all the movement of the tides and all the use and abuse it would receive at the hands of man and still make its way through the heavens exactly on time.

Listen, this is the One Who is planning your life! This is the One Who dwells within you and walks within you. When you join yourself to the Lord, you become one spirit with Him (1 Corinthians 6:17). And He doesn't change or shrink up His abilities so He could fit them inside you.

No, if you're a born-again, Holy Spirit-baptized believer, He is everything *in you* that He has ever been. He has the same awesome power. He has the same astounding ability to compute, to comprehend and plan in infinite detail everything that has ever been—everything that now is—and everything that ever will be!

What's more, when you run into something you can't handle and you call on Him for help, He's not a million light years away. He's right there inside you! He's ready to supply you with whatever you need.

He's ready to be your comforter. He's ready to be your teacher and your trainer. He's ready to be your advocate, your standby, your counselor. He's ready to put His supernatural power and mind to work for you 24 hours a day.

A Perfect Gentleman

"Well then, why hasn't He helped me before now?" you ask. *"Heaven knows I've needed it!"*

He's been waiting for you to give Him something He can work with. He's been waiting there inside you just like He hovered over the face of the waters in Genesis, waiting for you to speak the Word of God in faith.

That's been His role since the beginning - to move on God's Word and deliver the power necessary to cause that Word to manifest in the earth. That's what He did at creation...and that's what He is commissioned to do for you.

But remember, He's your helper, not your dominator. If you're walking around talking doubt, unbelief and other worthless junk, He is severely limited. He won't slap His hand over your mouth and say, "You dummy, I don't care what you say, I'm going to bless you anyway."

No, the Holy Spirit is the perfect gentleman. He'll never force anything on you. He'll just wait quietly for you to open the door for Him to work.

So decide right now to start opening that door. Develop an awareness of the reality of the Holy Spirit within you. Stop spending all your time meditating on the problems you're facing and start spending it meditating on the power of the One inside you Who can solve the problems. In other words, start becoming more God-inside minded!

Do you know what will happen if you do that? All heaven will break loose in your life.

The Holy Spirit Within

Instead of walking around moaning about how broke you are and how you can't afford to give much to spread the gospel, you'll start thinking about the fact that the One with the power to bring God's Word to pass is living inside you, and you'll change your tune. You'll start saying things like, "God meets my needs according to His riches in glory, so I have plenty to meet my own needs and give to every good work!"

Then the Holy Spirit within you will go into action. He'll give you plans, ideas and inventions. He'll open doors of opportunity and then give you the strength and ability to walk through them.

Instead of sitting around wishing there was something you could do for your sick, unsaved neighbor, you'll march into his house, tell him about Jesus, and then lay hands on him fully expecting the Holy Spirit within you to release God's healing power and cause him to recover.

Instead of sitting around simply admiring the works of Jesus and reading about them each Sunday in church, you'll hit the streets and do those works yourself—and even greater works (see John 14:12). You'll stand up boldly and say:

> *"The Spirit of the LORD is upon Me, Because He has anointed Me, To preach the gospel to the poor;*
> *He has sent Me to heal the brokenhearted,*
> *To proclaim liberty to the captives*
> *And recovery of sight to the blind*
> *To set at liberty those who are oppressed;*
> *To proclaim the acceptable year of the LORD"*
> Luke 4:18-19

More Than You Can Think

"Wait a minute. Jesus spoke those words about Himself!"

Yes, He did. But He also said, *"...As my Father hath sent me, even so send I you"* (John 20:21).

You've been sent just like Jesus was. You've been sent to your family, your neighborhood, your workplace, your world to deliver the burden-removing, yoke-destroying power of God!

That's the reason God baptized you in the Holy Spirit. He intended for you to walk into a place and bring the power of God on the scene—the same power that enabled Samson to defeat the Philistines and make a fool out of the devil! The same power that enabled Elijah to call down fire from heaven and outrun the fastest horses in the country! The same power that enabled Jesus to heal the sick, raise the dead and calm the sea!

Can you imagine what all God could do in this earth if we'd just become God-inside minded enough to let that power flow?

No, you can't. For as the Apostle Paul said, He is *"able to do exceedingly abundantly above all that we ask or think, according to the power that works in us"* (Ephesians 3:20).

Maybe you've been waiting for God to do something in your life or in the lives of those around you. Maybe you've been saying, *"I know God is able to change this situation. I wonder why He doesn't do it?"* If so, read that last phrase again. It says He is able to do above what we can ask or think *according to the power that works in you!*

Start building your faith in that power. Instead of always gazing toward heaven saying, *"God, why don't You help me?"* look at yourself in the mirror and say, "The Spirit of God is living in me today and I expect Him to do wise, wonderful, amazing and miraculous things through me!"

Instead of meditating on your problems and natural inadequacies, get out your Bible and study the acts of the Holy Spirit from Genesis to Revelation. Start meditating on the power and sufficiency of the *Greater One* who lives and walks within you every moment of every day!

When you begin to realize what a dynamite team you two really are, you'll blast off into the realm of exceedingly above all that you can ask or think—and the devil will never be able to catch you.

****

Forecast Confession for Healing

In the name of Jesus my Lord
I am now releasing my faith
By confessing that I am healed
by the stripes of Jesus
Christ has redeemed me
from the curse of sin, sickness and poverty!

Jesus bore my sorrows, fears, and pain.
The Lord has given me power, love,
and a sound mind.

I am strong in the Lord
And in the power of His might.

Lord, Your Words are healing and medicine
for my spirit, soul, and body.

Thank You Lord Jesus!

****

Forecast Confessions activate and develop our faith.
It's similar to pictures in a camera.
We already have the pictures captured.
But we will not actually possess a print,
until we develop them.

****

PERSONAL FORECAST STRATEGY 6

Cure For the Common Cold — Heart
(Tuning In to the Voice of God)

You probably know people who always seem very *cold* and negative about life. You have probably even said to them, *"how can you always seem to be so cold, uncaring, and negative?"*

It seems that this has become as common as a seasonal "cold" for so many people in the 21st century. There have been so many disappointments, hurts, and "bad breaks" that they have no hope, no real joy, and definitely no lasting peace. We are bombarded daily by the media with bad news, criticism, and news analysis. We have grown "cold" to godly living because even church-goers are just as "down-in-the-dumps" as everyone else in the world. It's so easy to "lose heart" and give up—taking the easy way of being led by our emotions, instead of the "higher" way—God's way.

But you don't have to lose heart! There's a cure for the common cold—heart!

The Spirit Is Trying to Lead

What is the Spirit of God saying to you today? Is the Holy Spirit trying to get through to you with a better way to live? What is He telling you about your spiritual development...your family...and your finances? If you're facing trouble, what word of victory has He spoken to you?

As a born-again child of the living God, you ought to know the answers to those questions.

I've learned by experience, however, the majority of believers don't. I can tell by just listening to them talk. *"Oh, no!"* they'll say, *"I'm in a crisis and I don't know what to do!"*

If that's your situation, I'm going to be straight with you. You'd better go to God and find out what to do. You'd better be quiet long enough to hear what He has to say and pay attention to it. You'd better get rid of that fear and start believing God. Otherwise, the devil is going to end up getting the best of you.

If you read the Bible you'll see that God has been trying to get His people to understand that for thousands of years. In fact He gave those exact instructions to an Old Testament king named Ahaz back in the days of the prophet Isaiah. Ahaz was in serious trouble at the time. He had two enemy armies coming against him and he had no idea what to do about it. So God sent His Word to Ahaz through the prophet Isaiah and gave him a whole new perspective.

Instead of agreeing with Ahaz about how powerful his enemies were, God let him know they didn't impress Him much. He referred to them as two *"smoking stumps"* (Isaiah 7:4, *The Amplified Bible*). Then He assured Ahaz their plans against him would not stand if he would simply obey the following instructions: *Take heed...be quiet...fear not* (verse 4)...and *believe* (verse 9).

Check Your Receiver

Before you head down the road looking for a prophet like Isaiah to tell you what God is saying to you, let me save you a trip. You don't need a prophet to tell you what to do. You have a better covenant than Ahaz had. You're not just a servant of God like people were in the Old Covenant. Through the blood of Jesus, you've become a full-fledged son and the Bible says, *"For as many as are led by the Spirit of God, they are the sons of God"* (Romans 8:14).

Jesus confirmed that fact in John 10 when He said that His *"sheep hear his voice; and he calls his own sheep by name and leads them out. And when he brings out his own sheep, he goes before them; and the sheep follow him, for they know his voice"* (John 10:3-4).

As a child of Almighty God, you have the right and the spiritual ability to hear the voice of God for yourself!

It's Comeback Time!

"But," you might say, *"God never speaks to me."* Sure He does. You're just not listening.

Have you ever turned on your television and found something was wrong with the picture? Maybe it was fuzzy or the sound was crackling with static. Or maybe you couldn't get a picture at all. Did you grab the telephone, call NBC and tell them that something was wrong with their transmitter? Did you get some television executive on the line and say, "Hey, you guys must not be broadcasting anymore. I turned on my set and you weren't there!"

Certainly not! That didn't even occur to you. You were smart enough to figure out the problem most likely wasn't with the transmitter. The problem was with the receiver. The problem was with your own television set.

So instead of blaming the broadcaster, you started trying to find the problem on your end. You might have checked the electrical connections. You might have looked to make sure the cable was hooked up. You might have checked the settings on the television to make sure they were all adjusted correctly.

What's more, you stayed with it until you got it fixed. Why? Because you never doubted the fact that the networks were still broadcasting. You understood if you could just get *tuned in*, they would be there for you.

Find His Frequency

Don't you think we ought to have at least as much faith in God as we have in the television networks? They can break down. They can fail us. But God never will. He has given us His Word. He has promised He'll lead us by His Spirit and enable us to know His voice. So if we're having difficulty with those things, we need to stop blaming Him and determine where we're missing it.

Actually, that's not hard to do. When we have trouble hearing God's voice it's almost always for one of the following four reasons.

1. We don't believe He is speaking.
2. We're not paying attention.

3. We're allowing some kind of interference.
4. We just plain don't know what frequency He is on.

Let's focus right now on that last point. Exactly how do you locate the frequency God uses to speak to you?

I'll tell you right off the bat, you don't do it by using those fleshly paddles on the sides of your head—your natural ears. Some people try to hear God that way. They think if He would just speak audibly to them everything would be solved.

They're mistaken. Our natural ears weren't designed to hear the voice of God.

We were created to hear Him in our inner man or what the New Testament calls *"the hidden man of the heart"* (1 Peter 3:4).

As Hebrews 3:7-8 says, *"Therefore, as the Holy Spirit says: Today, if you will hear His voice, Do not harden your hearts as in the rebellion In the day of trial in the wilderness."*

God leads His children not by outward voices or signs and wonders but by the inward witness of "the hidden man of the heart". So to find His frequency, the first thing you'll have to do is tune in—*not with your head but with your heart!*

Learn to Discern

How do you know the difference between your head and your heart?

Scripturally speaking, your head is your soul which is comprised of your mind, will and emotions. Your heart is your spirit which is the core of your being that has been born again and joined to the Spirit of God. Granted, discerning the difference between the voice of your soul and the voice of your spirit can be challenging and it takes spiritual wisdom to do it. But the Bible tells us clearly how to develop that wisdom: *We do it by spending time in the written Word of God.*

God's Words are not just ordinary words—they are alive and powerful.

"For the word of God is living and powerful, and sharper than any two-edged sword, piercing even to the division of soul and spirit, and of joints and marrow, and is a discerner of the thoughts and intents of the heart."

Hebrews 4:12

God always agrees with His written Word and His Word always agrees with Him. In fact, Psalm 138:2 says He has magnified His Word even above His Name. That means God has put His Name on His written Word the way we would put our name at the bottom of a contract. He has given us His Word as a covenant and signed it in the Name of Jesus by the blood of Jesus.

Since God cannot lie, there is no way He will ever do or say anything contrary to that Word. He has absolutely joined Himself to it forever. So, the first place God takes us to train us to recognize His voice, is to His written Word. He uses it to tune our spiritual ears to the real so that we can easily recognize a counterfeit.

You Will Know That You Know

Have you ever watched an impersonator mimic a celebrity? If he is good at what he does, you'll think, *I know who that guy is impersonating. It's so-and-so. He sounds just like him!* But if you were to put the real personality right next to the impersonator, the differences would be glaring. If you could see them both at the same time, you'd think, *That guy doesn't sound much like him at all!*

That's the way it is with God's written Word. The better you know it, the more you've heard God's voice speaking to you through it, the easier it is for you to tell the difference between His voice and another voice. The easier it is for you to divide your soul from your spirit and discern the difference between the voice of your head and the voice of your heart.

When you're trained to hear God's voice in His Word, the devil won't be able to sneak deceptions in on you, either. When he tries to razzle-dazzle you with some religious-sounding voice that says, *I love you, my son. But it's just not my will to heal you at this time,* you won't buy it. You'll rise up and say, *"That's not the voice of*

God. That's a lie from hell because it doesn't agree with the Word that says 'by His stripes ye were healed.'"

Let me warn you though, you won't get that kind of training just casually reading the Bible now and then. You won't get it by knowing generally what it says—or by mixing what it says with your own opinions. If you desire to truly learn to hear the voice of God in the Word.

You'll have to take heed to it. You'll have to meditate in the Word day and night—so that you learn to *"know that you know that you know—down deep in your "knower!"*

Zero In

Paying attention is more than just mentally assenting to a Scripture and saying, *"Oh yes, hallelujah. Amen."* To pay attention means to lock in on what's being said and make a firm decision that from now on, you will see this matter the way God sees it instead of the way you've always looked at it.

To do that, you'll have to do the second thing God told Ahaz to do. You'll have to be quiet. You'll have to shut out all the mental jabbering you've been doing, stop thinking about your own opinions and listen—really listen—to what the Word says.

Do you realize it's possible to read great quantities of Scripture and never really hear what God is saying in it? It's not only possible; people do it all the time. Here's how it happens. We'll read a verse or two and something in them will trigger another train of thought. We may start thinking about what Aunt Sally said about that Scripture. Or what Grandma used to say. Or we may even let our mind wander off on something else altogether—all the while we're still reading our Bible! We end up with only a vague idea of what we read because we weren't really paying attention to the Word, we were paying attention to our own thoughts.

Reading the Word of God that way is like shooting scattershot at a flock of birds—you don't ever hit anything. To hear the voice of God through His Word, you have to take aim and zero in on every word as you read it. Instead of just breezing through the Bible reading it like you'd read a novel or a history book, read it deliberately.

We meditate Scriptures by thinking about how it applies to every area of our life, all day long.

Meditate on it by asking yourself, *What does that mean to me? How does it change my life?* Ask the Lord to reveal specifically what He is saying through that Word to you.

Read every verse with the attitude that, *This is God speaking to me and I am going to do what He tells me to do.* Make a quality decision you're going to act on that Word as quickly as you would the word of your doctor, lawyer or a very close, trusted friend.

Determine in advance that you're not going to bend the Word to fit your lifestyle. On the contrary, you're going to bend your lifestyle to fit that Word. With that attitude, your spiritual ears will be open to hear whatever God has to say.

Fear Not!

"But, I'm afraid I'll do those things and I still won't be able to hear the voice of God."

Well, stop being afraid of that! *Fear not!*

Instead take a step of faith and believe what Jesus said. He said you're His sheep and you hear His voice. So stop doubting Him and calling Him a liar. Don't ever, ever, EVER again say, "I can't hear God's voice."

Start agreeing with Jesus. Start believing and agreeing with the Word. Say, "The Word says I can hear God's voice and I believe it! I do hear the voice of God!"

Then put your faith into action. Open the ears of your heart and start listening for the voice of the Spirit, especially when you're reading the Word. Pay attention not just to the activity in your brain but to the *quickenings* in your inner man (primarily the area just below your chin, or chest area).

If you're not sure where to locate those stirrings, just think back to a time when you had what we sometimes call a "hunch." Suddenly something just *dawned on* you and you knew or understood something you hadn't known before. Those kinds of *dawnings* come from your born-again spirit.

Make a decision to become more aware of the promptings that arise from your spirit because they are the leading of God. Learn to trust them. The Holy Spirit will help you to step out on them a little at a time.

Initially He won't be giving you risky, world-shaking kinds of leadings. When you're first learning to identify God's voice, it will be mostly yes and no answers, not to go sell everything you own and invest it in some off-the-wall business venture. He'll begin by showing you simple truths from the Word that you can act on. He'll reveal from the Word, for example, how you can obey more fully the law of love. He'll show you ways to bless the people around you.

The more you trust His voice and follow His leadings, the more clearly you'll find you can hear from Him. Before long, hearing from God won't be an occasional event but an everyday part of life. And when someone asks you, "What is the Spirit of God telling you today?" you won't hesitate a moment.

You'll know exactly what to say.

Making the Supernatural Your Natural

First Corinthians 2:9 says, *"Eye has not seen, nor ear heard, neither have entered into the heart of man, the things which God has prepared for them that love him."* God had tremendous things prepared for my life—things beyond my wildest imagination! I'm seeing them and enjoying them. It's been a wonderful journey, and God isn't finished with my life yet. He desires for me to continue to grow in Him and fulfill His plan in my life.

God has marvelous things planned not just for me, but for *you* and every other believer. He is a great planner. He plans His work and works His plan!

Our lives can and should be overflowing in the presence and power of God. As believers, the supernatural should be our natural! We ought to be doing "exploits" for God. And we can! There is, however, a condition. Daniel 11:32 tells us: *"The people that do know their God shall be strong, and do exploits."*

Know Your Power Source

If you have a desire to do big things, impossible things for God—the things He calls "exploits"—then you have to fully understand the prerequisites.

To start with, *you must know God*. That doesn't mean you just know about Him. *Knowing* Him means having an intimate relationship with Him. It means He is the first thing you think of when you open your eyes in the morning, and the last you think of when you go to bed at night. Listening to Him all day, every day, and letting Him talk to you through His written Word and by His Spirit is how you get to *know* Him. You come to really *know* the Lord by actively seeking Him above everything else and *recognizing Him as your source* (Matthew 6:31-33). And, as you begin to *know* Him—you will begin to know His power.

The Apostle Paul said having an intimate, living connection with Jesus was worth more than everything he had previously considered valuable. He said his *determined purpose* was to *know* Him. This is a purpose I've made my own, and it can be yours too.

> *"That I may know Him and the power of His resurrection, and the fellowship of His sufferings, being conformed to His death,"*
>
> Philippians 3:10

The Spirit of "Greater Works"

In this passage of Scripture, you can hear how deeply Paul desired the Lord and the power of His resurrection. Jesus told His disciples He wanted them to receive this power, to be "endued with power from on high." He gave them instructions to wait in Jerusalem until He sent the Holy Spirit for this purpose.

> *"Most assuredly, I say to you, he who believes in Me, the works that I do he will do also; and greater works than these he will do, because I go to My Father"*
>
> John 14:12

Greater works—exploits! That's what Jesus expects us to do. And we can when we yield to the Holy Spirit who dwells within us. Jesus knew His disciples had to have the Baptism in the Holy Spirit to do the mighty works God planned for them. That hasn't changed. Knowing Jesus as our Savior and being filled with the Spirit are still the first steps toward doing the impossible.

With God, All Things Are Possible

The truth is, God has a purpose for your life that's exciting and beyond anything you can imagine without the Holy Spirit revealing it. You may not feel able to do great things, but you can. Just realize God never intended you to do them on your own. God knows what He put in you and *what He can do in you.* Ephesians 3:20 says He is *"able to do exceedingly abundantly above all that we ask or think, according to the power that works in us."*

We in the Body of Christ are vessels that God works *through* to accomplish His will.

> *"We are His workmanship, created in Christ Jesus for good works, which God prepared beforehand that we should walk in them"*
>
> Ephesians 2:10

Helping others receive new life and victory through Christ should not be unusual for us. Remember we are working with God Himself. We should expect miracles!

Scripture reveals that truth over and over:

> *"…all things are possible to him who believes"*
>
> Mark 9:23

We have a vital relationship with the One who makes the impossible possible. The heroes of faith recorded in the Bible *knew* God, and they did impossible things. They *believed* God when He said, *"I will be with you."* (See Exodus 3:12; Isaiah 41:10.) Their faith was anchored on that promise. And because God *was* with them, they weren't limited to the natural realm.

The giants didn't matter to David—God was with him. The Flood didn't matter to Noah—God was with him. Age didn't matter to Abraham—God was with him.

He is still the God of the impossible! God is still with us. He has *planned* to do great things through each of us. When we truly get to know Him, we will trust Him, believe His Word and not be afraid to act on it. That's called walking by faith!

Become a Faith Giant

Faith—believing what God has said—is the foundation for a supernatural life. In John 6:28, the disciples asked Him, *"What shall we do, that we might work the works of God?"* Jesus answered in the next verse, *"This is the work of God, that ye believe on him whom he hath sent."*

The faith giants listed in Hebrews 11 accomplished great things *by faith*—by believing God. Verse 1 says, "Now faith is the substance of things hoped for, the evidence of things not seen." It is only *by faith* that what you're hoping for will manifest.

Today, your body may be sick or diseased, your finances may be in shambles, or your mind may be tormented by fear and worry. If so, I want you to know I understand what that feels like. And I also want you to know that you don't have to stay in that condition.

Before I began to know and believe the Word of God, those things imprisoned me—but I came out of it! And so can you, if you will get in the Word and learn the truth about all the great things that already belong to you in Christ.

I learned to stand on God's promises and appropriate them in our lives. *I believed I received what God said was already ours, and we talked like it and acted like it.* And, the truth of the Word made us free.

Never will you find in the Bible where God wanted His people to be poor, sick or defeated. Never! Never! Never! It didn't happen. The only reason God's people have been broke, disgusted, sorry and sick is because they didn't do what He said—they didn't do things His way.

It's easy to coast along and be like everybody else. But if you truly desire to be a faith giant and do exploits for God, you have to believe His Word. If you'll believe His Word and do things His way, the supernatural can be your natural.

One Flash of Power

All it takes is one flash of light from the Word to change your life forever. One flash of faith and you will realize, *God said I can have that!* As you speak that promise, it will become more real to you than anything else. That's when you have the victory on the *inside*—that's when the natural realm must respond. That's when the supernatural becomes natural.

None of us can afford to be lazy about the Word of God. Our future is tied up in how much Word we have in our hearts.

That's why God said,

"My son, give attention to my words; Incline your ear to my sayings. Do not let them depart from your eyes; Keep them in the midst of your heart; For they are life to those who find them, And health to all their flesh. Keep your heart with all diligence, For out of it spring the issues of life"
Proverbs 4:20-23

It's up to us how much of the power of God we experience. As we feed on the Word, speak it and act on it, the Word will become a reality to us and the power in God's Word *will* drive out fear, failure and sickness!

At one point in my Christian life I let my hunger for the Word of God decrease instead of increase. Too much of my attention was going toward natural things. The truth is, I had gotten comfortable in life. We had nice cars, a decent house, a little money in the bank— we just weren't as excited as we once had been.

But, after I began to diligently start every morning with a *"Breakfast of Champion's"* prayer to ask for the Holy Spirit's leading, I refocused my attention! *(See this prayer at the end of "Personal Forecast Strategy 3".)*

I felt strongly that the Holy Spirit began to silently speak: *"Purpose in your heart that you'll not be lazy, that you'll not draw back, hold back or sit down, but purpose in your heart that you'll rise up and march forward and become on fire."*

I'm determined to be strong and do His exploits!

How about you?

Soar in the Spirit

We know too that "doing exploits" also requires laying aside every weight and sin that can hinder us (Hebrews 12:1). Weights are things that hold us down in the natural realm—things that crowd our hearts and take our focus and energy away from the things of God.

Mark 4 gives a good list of those things. Although cares, distractions and desire for other things are not necessarily sin, they are things that will hold us down to the natural realm. And, when the natural man, "the flesh," is in control, faith loses its aggressiveness.

But why would anyone choose to live in the natural realm, on a low, low level, when we can live in the supernatural realm and soar in the spirit?

With the help of the Holy Spirit you can *"crucify"* the flesh (Galatians 5:24) and renew your mind to the Word (Romans 12:2). You can be *"spiritually minded"* and experience life and peace. Or you can be "naturally" or "carnally minded" and think like the world thinks, and get what the world gets—death (see Romans 8:6).

Your spirit—the part of you that is connected to God—can always be in command. When that's the case, it isn't difficult to receive the wisdom or help you need to overcome any situation. When you are vitally connected to the God of the impossible, it becomes easy for the supernatural to thrive.

You can live a limited life in the earth—limited to your natural ability and circumstances—or you can live unlimited. It's your choice, just like it was Israel's choice. They had to decide if they were going to follow after God, or settle for the natural things in the world and live like the heathen people around them.

Put Your Foot on the Promise

At one point in particular, they chose wrong. When God told the children of Israel to take the Promised Land, they *forgot who was with them* and saw only their own inabilities.

That generation did *not* take the land God said He had given to them. They refused to possess—or put their foot on—the land God had promised them.

But in Joshua 1:3, when God told Joshua, *"Every place that the sole of your foot shall tread upon, that have I given unto you,"* Joshua believed Him. Notice God didn't say, I'm *going to give* it to you. He said, every place you put your foot, I *have given* to you—past tense. If Joshua hadn't picked up his foot and put it down on that property—on that promise—he wouldn't have received it.

But Joshua did! The people were with him, and together they took the land. Joshua did what God told him, when He told him.

"March around the walls seven times and then shout."

And they did. If their hearts had been hardened like the previous generation, they would not have obeyed God. It took God-inspired courage to do that, and they had hearts toward God. What happened? God took action, and suddenly they weren't limited to the natural realm. Miraculously the walls fell flat. The Israelites possessed their land.

When a miracle was needed, God performed a miracle.

That's the way God desires the Church to live—believing Him for the supernatural. Today we're at the same place Joshua was. *God had already given him the land, but he had to act on what God said.* God has told us things in His Word that belong to us. We have to put our foot on them and possess them. We have to walk out on the Word.

I believe we're at the place and the hour where modern day prophecy is being fulfilled. The Lord is recruiting an army of believers to do what He wants done in the earth. But He isn't looking for *lukewarm* Christians.

He is looking for those who will purpose in their hearts not to be lazy, draw back, hold back or sit down. He is looking for those who will rise up, march forward, be on fire!

He is looking for you and me to make a determination to know our God and do exploits! He is waiting to make the supernatural our natural.

Experience the Fullness of the Holy Spirit

After you make Jesus the Lord of your life, it is the will of God that you experience the fullness of the Holy Spirit. Ephesians 5:18 says, *"And be not drunk with wine, wherein is excess; but be filled with the Spirit."*

It is the Holy Spirit's ministry not only to impart the nature of God to the spirit of man at salvation, but to come and live in the new creature. His job is to reveal the exact knowledge of God from the heart of the Father. A believer cannot understand, by his own spirit alone, the profound wisdom of God. This is why Jesus said in John 14:26 that the Father would send us the Comforter to teach us "all things."

When you receive the Holy Spirit, you receive the ability of God. Acts 1:8 says, *"But you shall receive power when the Holy Spirit has come upon you."*

The word *power* in that verse is translated *dunamis*, which means ability and might. It is through the energizing force of the Holy Spirit living in us that we are transformed into effective witnesses. So, to be born again and not filled with the Spirit is like being a train without a track.

The ability you receive to pray with your spirit when you are baptized in the Holy Spirit is powerful. It edifies and builds up your spirit man and puts you in contact with the deep things of God (1 Corinthians 14:4, 2:10). It also allows you to pray God's perfect will apart from your natural understanding and aids you in interceding for others (Romans 8:26-27). And according to Jude 1:20-21, praying in the Spirit strengthens and intensifies your personal relationship with God.

The Power of the Holy Spirit Is For Everyone

The promise of receiving the Holy Spirit is for everyone in the Body of Christ because God gave His Spirit to the Church on the Day of Pentecost (Acts 2:32-33, 39). As a partaker of your covenant with God, however, you must individually receive what He has given you.

When you ask for the indwelling of the Holy Spirit, the Word of God promises that you shall receive.

> *"So I say to you, ask, and it will be given to you; seek, and you will find; knock, and it will be opened to you. For everyone who asks receives, and he who seeks finds, and to him who knocks it will be opened. If a son asks for bread from any father among you, will he give him a stone? Or if he asks for a fish, will he give him a serpent instead of a fish? Or if he asks for an egg, will he offer him a scorpion? If you then, being evil, know how to give good gifts to your children, how much more will your heavenly Father give the Holy Spirit to those who ask Him!"*
>
> Luke 11:9-13

Throughout the New Testament, when believers received the Holy Spirit, they began to speak in a heavenly language. Acts 2:4 says, *"And they were all filled with the Holy Ghost, and began to speak with other tongues, as the Spirit gave them utterance."*

This is still true today. When you accept the Spirit's indwelling, your spirit will immediately have a desire to express itself in praise to God. The Holy Spirit will give utterance through you as you give Him permission.

When you pray in tongues, you are praying in the Spirit.

You are letting the Holy Spirit pray through your spirit.

The Amplified Bible says in 1 Corinthians 14:14, *"My spirit [by the Holy Spirit within me] prays...."*

Just as your native language is the voice of your mind, your prayer language is the voice of your spirit.

If you desire the infilling of the Holy Spirit or if you are unsure whether you have received it, say the prayer below:

Heavenly Father, I am a new creation in Christ. Please fill me with Your Holy Spirit to enable me to be a powerful witness of Jesus. I believe that I now receive the Holy Spirit just as the disciples did on the day of Pentecost. In Jesus' mighty name!

****

Forecast Confession for Abiding In the Word of Christ

Jesus is Lord of my life.
Therefore, I am determined to abide in His Words.
I let the Word of Christ dwell in me richly.
As I continue to *hear* the Word of Christ,
and remain faithful to be a *doer* of the Word;
It will be as if I have built my life on the solid Rock.

When the storms of life rage against me,
and try to bring me down;
I will not fall—I will not be defeated,
for my life is built on the solid Rock.

The "Word" is spirit and life to me.
The "Word" is faith food for my *spiritman*.
Therefore, my spirit takes charge
of my soul and body.
When I speak the Word,
in the mighty name of Jesus,
My victory is already won.

Thank You Lord!

****

PERSONAL FORECAST STRATEGY 7

You Are the Prophet In Your Own Life
(Prophesy Life to the Dry Bones)

I can still see the discouraged faces of hundreds of men standing around in the prison courtyard. It was 1973 and I was playing baseball for a Detroit Federation, class "A" baseball team. We were at Jackson State Prison to play a game against the inmates. They had a great Baseball team that year—one player had actually signed a major league contract to play with the Detroit Tigers.

When I think back to the hundreds of faces I saw that day, I remember the look of hopelessness. It's that "all too familiar" look of disappointment and discouragement. It's that look of "settling" for a future that will be just as hopeless as today.

Another tragedy is that I see that same look on the faces of many people that I pass on the street, in the malls, and in restaurants today. People have been "lulled" into passivity by the media, and always expect the worse to happen. The truth is that "sometimes" we "ask" for it. We actually "talk" ourselves into receiving the negative, doubt-filled, depressing thoughts of defeat just like the devil wants us to do.

Personal Prophecy

Believe it or not—you are making a *"personal forecast"* for your future with your own words! When you consider your everyday life as a Spirit-filled believer—you are the "prophet" of your own life.

God has given us the power to choose words that directly influence our future—for good or for bad. We can speak positive words of faith and expect God's blessing, or we can choose negative words and expect things to go wrong. Our own words become a personal forecast for the future.

Thousands of years ago the Lord had specific instructions for people who were facing a bleak future. In the book of Ezekiel we can read how the Lord instructed His people to "speak life" to their challenging circumstances. He gave a vivid illustration of "prophesying" life to the "dry, dead bones." (See Ezekiel 37.)

Prophets and Prophecy

The prophets of the Old Covenant, (before Christ redeemed mankind), prophesied about the days we are living in. This is an awesome time to witness what the Lord is doing in the earth at the *"end of the ages."*

The Lord God has always desired a personal communication with His creation. All through the ages God has spoken through prophets to release His people from crisis situations. He has given His Word to teach people how to be free from bondage, fear, sickness, and sorrow.

There are at least 100 confirmed words of prophecy concerning Christ our Lord — and that is in addition to the hundreds of prophetic words throughout the Holy Bible concerning specific people, places, and events. *(God's Word is awesome!)*

In the New Covenant, prophecy and the ministry gifts have "continued" in a far more personal way. The ministry gifts — apostles, prophets, evangelists, pastors, and teachers — have been given to build up every believer to be able to fulfill their individual gifts, and teach them the power of their own words. (Ephesians 4:11.)

In the Old Covenant, (before Christ), the Holy Spirit was given to one single prophet who spoke prophecy to the people on specific occasions. But in the New Covenant, the Holy Spirit has been poured out on all people, so that they will be able to stand strong in their own personal confession of faith.

The voice of the prophet was established as God's primary method of communication with His people. It was this prophetic communication anointing that enabled Adam, Enoch, Noah,

Abraham, Isaac, Jacob, Moses, and others to predict future events. This is how they received instruction from God concerning how they would be blessed, deliverance from bondage, and the prophecies that predicted and prepared the way of the coming Messiah.

Personal Prophecy

Don't misunderstand—when I say *"you are the prophet in your own life"*—I'm not saying that we all have the "ministry gift of a Prophet." Definitely not!

We should all desire spiritual gifts, especially the gift of prophecy. But there is a difference between the "general" prophecy that I refer to when making a "forecast confession" of God's Word—and the "specific and personal" words from a believer flowing with the "gift of prophecy."

In one sense the whole Bible can correctly be called "prophecy"—because God is communicating His thoughts and Will to mankind.

The Greek word, "logos" refers to the totally complete, creative, infallible Word of God; the Scriptures, the Holy Bible. (2 Timothy 3:16.) It also refers to Jesus as the eternal, complete Word of God, who was revealed and manifest in mortal flesh. (John 1:1-14.)

The Greek word, "rhema" is a "spoken word from the Word"—as referred to in Ephesians 6:17 and Romans 10:17. It's a "right on time" revealed portion of the whole Word of God.

We become "the prophet in our own lives" when we claim several specific Scriptures from the Logos Word as our own "personal" forecast confession. We are flowing with the "spiritual gift" of prophecy when we are inspired by the Holy Spirit with a specific Rhema Word for "someone else."

Your Personal Forecast

In an overall sense, you and I "are" what we are today—and we "have" what we have today—because of what we have said about ourselves yesterday. *(We were created that way.)*

Continually meditating on negative thoughts builds doubt and unbelief in your spirit until it overflows into a defeated attitude. Then it is released in words of fear and worry.

The Bible kind of *"personal forecast"* is activated when you and I pray and speak God's powerful, "Omnipotent" Words. This transforms "our" natural words of prayer into powerful and "potent" words that will win personal victories in life!

A Bible *forecast* is based on what God can do and what Jesus has already done for us. It's making a declaration such as, *"I can do all things through Christ who strengthens me,"* (Philippians 4:13). And, *"The Lord is on my side—I will not fear,"* (Psalm 118:6).

The word *forecast* is a synonym for familiar Bible words, like: profess, confess, prophesy, foretell, and predict. Your *personal forecast* should be saying and praying God's Word.

It is important to realize that your *personal forecast* should be entirely based on a positive-faith attitude about God's Word and Will. It is never a personal boast, or an untrusting, fear about the future.

Your *personal forecast* of God's promises is a way to believe for the promises of God even when you don't feel good enough, when you think you have failed at life, when you feel depressed, sick, angry, or stressed out.

What You *"Say"* Is a *Forecast Confession*

We can talk about feeling full of worry, failure, and sickness—or we can talk about the way God can turn things around and His goodness into our lives. Either way, our words are *forecasting* what we expect and believe for our future.

Your *personal forecast*, or *confession of faith* is thankful and bold believing and receiving of God's promises. We can learn to agree with God's Word that says we are *"overcomers"* and *"more than conquerors"* in Christ Jesus! (See 1 John 5:4 and Romans 8:37.)

"Confession" is a principle that is found throughout the Bible. A confession of what you believe in your heart, works just as sure as the principles of gravity or electricity.

If we look closely at the way God has created everything, it is apparent that God did not merely *describe* the darkness He saw.

God used His words to *change* what He saw. He spoke light into existence. He spoke the heavens and the earth into existence. (See Genesis 1:1-14.)

You might be thinking, *Yes, but that was God, and I am not God.*

You are absolutely right! But according to the apostle Paul, we are to *follow* and be *imitators* of God. (See 1Corinthians 11:1 and Ephesians 5:1.)

What Is Your Confession?

Confessing God's Word is admitting that God's Word is true. It's agreeing with the Bible!

All too often our confession is based on our physical senses: what we see, how we feel, or what the circumstances are. Rather than saying how you feel, say what God's Word says about you.

By confessing the powerful Word of God, we are receiving the blessings that God has already provided in His Word of promise.

Your forecast confession is what and who you are "becoming" in Christ.

Some people wake up every morning and groan, "Oh, no, it's morning again." Other people declare, *"Good morning, Lord. I believe something good is going to happen today!"*

Say what you want, not what you have. Sometimes we have thoughts and feelings of being a failure, but by speaking the Word we can look beyond our feelings.

Here's a great Bible truth: *"Let the weak say, 'I am strong' "* (Joel 3:10).

God does not expect us to deny our troubled circumstances. But if we continuously complain about our problems, we are destined to make things worse. Confessing God's Word will change our circumstances.

How to Overcome Trouble

Trials and tragedies have no respect for background, status, or financial position. The storms of life hit everyone: rich, poor, strong, weak, good, bad, intellectual, lonely, or famous.

Jesus said: *"In the world you will have tribulation; but be of good cheer, I have overcome the world,"* (John 16:33).

The Bible gives us the way to have this overcoming victory: *"They overcame him by the blood of the Lamb and by the word of their testimony,"* (Revelation 12:11).

Praying and speaking the Word of God can overcome the problems, hurts, and challenges of life that the devil has meant for harm and destruction.

According to Matthew 12:34, whatever is in your heart in abundance is what you believe and talk about. And whatever you pray and say will directly affect your life—you'll have what you say! (See Mark 11:23-24.)

The Most Powerful Force In the Universe

There is nothing that we have, or will have, that is more powerful than our words. *"Death and life are in the power of the tongue,"* (Proverbs 18:21). God created us that way!

Almighty God could have chosen to swing His arm to create the universe.

He could have just had a thought and there would have been a world. But He chose His words and He said, *"Let there be light,"* and there was light.

Consider our prayers to God. He already knows our needs and desires. But there is something vitally important about expressing our thoughts by the spoken word.

Words of prayer, (if it's according to the Word) carry the will of God to the earth. That is why the book of James teaches that we do not have because we do not ask, (James 4:2).

Many people go along day after day hoping nothing bad will happen that they cannot handle. Then, when something does happen, they try to change things with a few moments of prayers and tears.

The reality is that they might have been *forecasting* what happened by putting spiritual laws into motion.

How do we put spiritual laws into motion? Through the words we speak day after day.

Jesus taught that we can speak to mountains; (problems). We can tell them to *"be removed and be cast into the sea,"* and if we speak and do not doubt in our hearts, but believe that what we say will be done, we will have whatever we say; "forecast." (See Mark 11:22-25.)

We should talk "to" the problem—not "about" the problem.

The overall Bible truth is that, "We will never rise above our *forecast* confession of faith.

Faith Is Confidence In God's Ability

If you understand the way fear works, you can see why Jesus warned us so sternly against it. Fear is the opposite of faith.

Faith is confidence in God's ability to protect you. Fear is confidence in the enemy's ability to hurt you.

In the same way faith opens the door for God to bring blessings into your life, fear opens the door for the devil to bring destruction.

When Jesus said we are not to let our hearts be troubled, He wasn't telling us to stick our heads in the sand and pretend the trouble isn't there.

He wasn't telling us to ignore the events around us. Look at what He said in John's gospel: *"Let not your heart be troubled; you believe in God, believe also in me,"* (John 14:1).

Jesus also said, *"These things I have spoken to you, that in Me you may have peace. In the world you will have tribulation; but be of good cheer, I have overcome the world,"* (John 16:33).

The secret to maintaining a confident heart in the midst of troubled times is to believe Jesus and His word of overcoming victory. Put more faith in what He said than in what the ungodly influences say.

The apostle Paul described confident faith like this:

"Now may the God of hope fill you with all joy and peace in believing, that you may abound in hope by the power of the Holy Spirit"

Romans 15:13

There Is a Miracle in Your Mouth

Your destiny is to know and experience the goodness of God. He created you with faith to overcome whatever comes your way in this life. God has given faith to every person—it is your job to believe. Throughout the ministry of Christ, He consistently promised that all things would be possible to anyone who believes. (See Matthew 19:26.)

You may be homeless, sick, or bruised from past experiences, but God can make a way for you to break free. You can be all God created you to be.

You may be successful and prosperous, but God has more for you to do. If you have another breath to take, your destiny is not yet complete. You can do more of the works and wonders of Christ and make a difference in this world.

To get an idea of how powerful our words can be, let's look at the book of James.

"If anyone does not stumble in word, he is a perfect man, able also to bridle the whole body. Indeed, we put bits in horses' mouths that they may obey us, and we turn their whole body. Look also at ships: although they are so large and are driven by fierce winds, they are turned by a very small rudder wherever the pilot desires,"

James 3:2-4

The book of James explains that the condition of our bodies can be turned, or guided, by our tongues. James leaves no question as to the power we have in our words.

But that power can either work for us or work against us. Either way, we are the ones who decide, because we are the pilots of our lives.

We have the power of choice to *forecast* a better life or *forecast* a dismal future with our own words. The tongue sets the course for our lives.

"The tongue is a fire, a world of iniquity. The tongue is so set among our members that it defiles the whole body, and sets on fire the course of nature; and it is set on fire by hell."
James 3:6

Our words can be a powerful tool used in our favor or they can also be an unruly and deadly force, causing our lives to be shipwrecked if we let them run out of control.

Our only hope for taming our tongues, and thereby charting a good course for our future, is the Word of God.

The Good Treasure

If we are going to use the Word of God to navigate through this life, there are a couple of issues we need to settle first.

How about those times when things are just not going your way? It may be in the area of marriage, finances, health, or work. Whatever it is, pressure seems to keep building until you feel like you're going to explode if you don't say something negative about it. (Which, in effect, is the way we *open the door* to "more" trouble.)

Why do you think it's so hard to keep our mouths under control in situations like that?

Jesus addressed this in the forth chapter of Mark. He warned that Satan comes to steal the Word of God from our hearts through tribulation, persecution, the cares of this world, the lust of other things, and deceitfulness of riches. He uses everything in this natural realm to stir up our flesh and get us to open our mouths to receive more trouble. (See Mark 4:14-20.)

So the issue comes down to this: What kind of words will we believe and speak?

The Bible explains it like this:

"For out of the abundance of the heart the mouth speaks. A good man out of the good treasure of his heart brings forth good things, and an evil man out of the evil treasure brings forth evil things,"

(Matthew 12:34-5).

It's not surprising that when we're under pressure from our flesh—being moved by what we see, feel, or think—we tend to open our mouths and say things like:

"I'm so unworthy," "I'm so tired," "I'm so broke," "I'm so ugly," and "I'm going nowhere in life!"

When the pressure is on, that's when we find out what's really inside us. It should be the Word of God. Right?

Heaven Backs Your Words

When you received Jesus as your Lord and Savior, it wasn't God talking to you that got you born again. It was "you" talking to God. You heard the gospel, and faith rose within your heart. Then you confessed it with your mouth, and the Holy Spirit performed a "new birth" of your spiritman!

The *new birth* happens when we pray according to the Word of God. The same holds true for any area of our lives. Power comes when we pray and confess the Word. (See Romans 10:8-10.)

But there's something else we need to factor into our power-filled words.

You and I have a priest we can go to—and He's not just any priest. We have Jesus, our heavenly High Priest. *"Consider the Apostle and High Priest of our confession, Christ Jesus,"* (Hebrews 3:1).

God sent Jesus to be High Priest over our words of faith. That's why we should always make sure our "words" and "prayers" agree with what the Lord has already said and done.

Jesus is not going to speak words for us and have them come to pass in our lives. No, He has already spoken. So what can you and I do?

First, stop saying the same things the world says, like, *"Nothing good ever happens to me,"* or, *"I'm sick and tired of this or that."*

We expect people of this world to say things like that. That's exactly what they can expect in a life without Jesus. (But not us!)

If we believe that our words determine our future health, wealth, and place in eternity, we need to stop rehearsing what we don't want and start talking what we do want.

Second, we need to start filling our mouths with the Word of God. Make a *forecast* confession such as, *"I will say of the Lord, 'He is my refuge and my fortress; My God, in Him will I trust',"* (Psalm 91:2-3).

The challenge for us is to change from worldly, negative words to positive words of God's truth.

Start creating a better world for yourself today. Begin by speaking strong words that are for God, not against Him. Speak words that your High Priest can honor and then bring to pass.

You'll See It When You Believe It

The vast majority of people, including believers, don't know how to control the words that come out of their mouths.

Letting our words fly is the worst thing we can do when our lives seem out of control. Curses fly when we are in pain. Lies fly when we're trying to cover sin. Gossip flies when we try to make others think we are in control of our lives.

Murmuring and complaining are sometimes our substitutes for a good forecast of faith.

Letting words fly is a *forecast* of failure. Your words work in the negative as sure as they work in the positive. Courageous words of faith in the face of any circumstance will produce the blessings of God.

A New Vision of Yourself

"It's Comeback Time" is a commitment to change the way you think about yourself. You can begin to see your future with spiritual "eyes of faith." You see yourself the way God sees you.

The *"eyes of faith"* is an expression used to describe a vision (dream) we have in our spirit.

It's Comeback Time!

After my father taught me how to hit a fastball, my dream grew into hitting a homerun. I began to foresee myself, with the eye of faith, hitting homeruns. (I actually hit a few too.) I had new thoughts about my potential abilities in baseball.

Although I did not inherit great natural abilities, I was a fairly good baseball player. I practiced diligently to develop skills as a center fielder. It quickly became apparent that the key to success was *anticipating* where the ball might be going before it was hit. I don't know how many times I chased a fly ball across center field. Certainly hundreds.

In time I knew as soon as the ball left the bat where it was going and where I had to be to intersect its flight before it hit the ground.

It's Comeback Time is all about exercising your faith to believe you are changing before you actually "see" any change. It's just like participating in any athletic competition. Athletes see a goal, they see a finish line, and they see themselves as winners before it happens.

When you were born again, you were re-created by God. A change took place. Your spirit became alive and one with God. You are now "in Christ." You may not look any different on the outside, but your spirit is brand new. Now you can see God's plan with the eyes of faith.

The new birth that occurred in you, when you accepted Jesus as your Lord by faith, was done by the creative power of God. It took place inside you—in your spirit.

Consider Jesus to be the High Priest of your confession, the One given full responsibility and all the resources of heaven to see that your words—His Word spoken out of your mouth—will come to pass in the earth. Consider Him! (Hebrews 3:1.)

It's Right Below Your Nose

Your *personal forecast*, or *confession of faith*, is never a personal boast, or a worried concern about the future. It's thankful and bold believing and receiving of God's promises in your life.

Sometimes we need to deal with the past in order to progress toward our God-given destiny. That's why one of the key foundations for this book is, *"Forgetting those things which are behind and reaching forward to those things which are ahead, I press toward the goal for the prize of the upward call of God in Christ Jesus,"* (Philippians 3:13-14).

You might be thinking: *Why would God want to bless my future? Why should I reach for the best I can be in Christ?*

God wants to bless you abundantly to establish His covenant (promises and divine plan) in the earth. God wants you to have a blessed life so you can help others realize their destiny in Christ, help the poor and suffering, and encourage others in godly living. (See Psalm 35:27.)

God has granted to us a phenomenal power in our words. We can speak great blessing and healing for our lives—and the lives of everyone we meet.

Don't just report on the past, or what you have and see today—pray, talk about, and *forecast* what you need from God's Word for today and tomorrow.

You might be thinking, *if words are so important, I will have to be perfect in everything I say!*

Jesus is the only one who is perfect. Our challenge is to diligently follow Him and learn the lessons He taught.

Being imperfect is something I know a lot about. But I also know where the target is.

It's right below your nose.

It's Comeback Time!

****

8 Strategies to Help You Make a Strong Comeback & Overcome Set-backs

1. Stir Yourself Up!
   It's Comeback Time – Decision Time

2. Take It By Force!
   Overcome the Past with Strong Faith

3. How To Walk On Water
   Aggressively Living by Faith

4. Who's The Boss?
   A New Beginning – Let Your Spirit Rule

5. Activate the Power of the Holy Spirit
   Surrender Your Will to God's Ways

6. Cure For the Common *Cold – Heart*
   Tuning in to the Voice of God

7. You Are the Prophet In Your Own Life
   Prophesy Life to the Dry Bones

8. The Word Will Make You Free
   How to overcome doubt

****

PERSONAL FORECAST STRATEGY 8

The Word Will Make You Free
(How to Overcome Doubt)

Many people have been doing things backward! Sometimes we have thought, *"If I could just kick this smoking habit, if I could just get rid of this disease, if I could only stop this addictive behavior, if I could just get some money in the bank—then I'd be free."*

But what we need to go after is the freedom first. Once we lay hold of real freedom, those cigarettes, that disease and that financial lack will fall powerless at our feet. They'll have no more ability to bind us than they had to bind Jesus.

You may say, *"Yeah, but people have prayed for me to get me that freedom—and I still don't have it."*
Jesus did not say that praying would make you free. He said you'd know the truth, and the truth would make you free! He said continue in My Word and you'll be free like Me! Get in the Word and act on it. Then the laying on of hands will work.

> *"If you abide in My word, you are My disciples indeed. 32 And you shall know the truth, and the truth shall make you free."*
>
> John 8:31-32

God's Word is truth (John 17:17) and His Word is far more powerful than just natural truth. Yet even natural truth can make you free to a certain extent. If someone taught you from the time you were a child, for instance, that two plus two is three, and you grew up believing that lie, it would keep you in bondage all your life. Every time you went to the store, you'd say, *"I want two of those and two of these."*

The clerk would grin and answer, *"Okay, here's three."* Then he'd charge you for four—and you'd let him do it because you wouldn't know any better.

You'd come out all your life one apple short or one orange short. You'd always be paying extra. You'd be in captivity to anyone who wanted to cheat you until some good-hearted person called you in and said, *"Hey, I don't know who told you two plus two is three, but it's been costing you a fortune. The truth is two plus two is four!"*

Some people have been taught a lie about the power of God's Word to give you a "comeback" victory over sin, sickness, and the devil. People have been told that some of God's Word has passed away with the apostles, some have been told that praying God's Word might not work for you.

The truth is that God's Word will work for you if you work it!

Overcoming Doubt

No one is immune to doubt. It can and does happen to us all. You've just got to know how to handle it when it comes. Even the greatest men and women of God recorded in the Bible had to deal with doubt. Jesus said of John the Baptist, *"Assuredly, I say to you, among those born of women there has not risen one greater than John the Baptist; but he who is least in the kingdom of heaven is greater than he"* (Matthew 11:11).

That means John was greater in the sight of Jesus than Abraham, Joseph, Moses, David, or any Old Testament character you can name. Yet John doubted the most important thing of all by questioning whether Jesus was really the Christ.

John the Baptist had been cast into prison for criticizing Herod about marrying his brother's wife, an incestuous relationship. He had been there sometime between six months and two years and became so discouraged that he asked two of his disciples to go to Jesus and ask Him if He really was the Christ. It's easy to read that and not think much about it, but the truth is, it was nothing but unbelief on the part of John the Baptist.

Think about who John was. He was separated unto God and filled with the Holy Spirit while he was still in the womb. Even Jesus wasn't filled with the Holy Spirit from the womb. It is believed he lived in the desert near the Dead Sea with the Essens, the writers of the Dead Sea Scrolls. They were a people who were super-legalistic who dogmatically practiced many rituals of self denial. He certainly had not lived what we would call an easy life. John was separated and focused on his purpose.

His entire life was committed to preparing the way for the Christ. He spent thirty years preparing for a ministry that would only last six short months. John is the one who saw Jesus and said, *"Behold! The Lamb of God who takes away the sin of the world!"* John 1:29).

God had revealed to him that through a visible sign from heaven he would know who the Christ was. He would see the Spirit of God descending upon the Messiah in bodily shape as a dove. That came to pass when John baptized Jesus in the Jordan River.

At that time, John was absolutely certain that Jesus was the Christ. He had zero doubt. He was so adamant about it that he said.

Anyone Can Doubt

After being imprisoned for a period of time, John the Baptist began to doubt. This says a number of things, but an important one is the fact that *anyone can doubt*. How did Jesus respond to John's doubt? Well, He certainly didn't respond the way most of us do. He told John's disciples to go back and tell him of the miracles they had witnessed and that John would be blessed if he would just believe. That's it. Jesus didn't try and make John feel better by letting him know He understood his pain or by making a few complimentary comments. Jesus reserved those comments till after John's disciples left (Luke 7:24-28).

This puzzled me for many years. Why didn't Jesus say these things about John the Baptist in the hearing of John's disciples so they could have brought him that word? It seemed to me like that would have helped John more than just telling him to look at the miracles, and he'll be blessed if he believes.

The Scriptures give us the answer.

> *"Then the eyes of the blind shall be opened, and the ears of the deaf shall be unstopped. Then shall the lame man leap as an hart, and the tongue of the dumb sing: for in the wilderness shall waters break out, and streams in the desert"*
>
> Isaiah 35:5-6

Jesus had already explained this same answer to John's messengers.

> *Jesus answered and said to them, "Go and tell John the things you have seen and heard: that the blind see, the lame walk, the lepers are cleansed, the deaf hear, the dead are raised, the poor have the gospel preached to them. 23 And blessed is he who is not offended because of Me."*
>
> Luke 7:22-23

Jesus' Method of Dealing with Doubts

Jesus performed all the miracles Isaiah prophesied He would do, and threw in the healing of a leper and raising someone from the dead just for good measure. What Jesus did was He perfectly fulfilled the prophecy about Himself, and then referred John the Baptist back to that word. Jesus reminded John of the Scriptures, to deal with his doubts. That's Jesus' method of dealing with our doubts.

Many of us have Bibles lying around gathering dust. Some of us even carry one. But when we're struggling with unbelief, we don't want a Scripture; we want something tangible, something emotional that we can feel.

But overcoming doubt isn't just about feeling better; it's about getting back into faith that only comes from the Word of God.

Jesus sent the Word back with John's disciples. He knew this would stir up John's spirit to overcome the doubt.

The only sure way to overcome doubt is to place your faith in the Word of God. Don't allow your five senses to dominate your thinking. You must come to a place to where God's Word is more real to you than anything you can see, taste, hear, smell, or feel. When you're in doubt, refer back to the Word of God just the way Jesus told John the Baptist to do. *(Faith comes by hearing and hearing by the Word.)*

The Strongest Kind of Faith

There are only two times recorded in the Bible when Jesus marveled at anything. Once He marveled at the people's great unbelief (Mark 6:6), and in Matthew 8:10 He marveled at a Gentile soldier's great faith. A faith that made Jesus marvel is worth examining. What was different about it?

The number one difference was what the centurion said.

The centurion answered and said, "Lord, I am not worthy that You should come under my roof. But only speak a word, and my servant will be healed. For I also am a man under authority, having soldiers under me. And I say to this one, 'Go,' and he goes; and to another, 'Come,' and he comes; and to my servant, 'Do this,' and he does it."
Matthew 8:8-9

The centurion had a faith that was in God's Word alone. He didn't have to have Jesus come to his house and wave His hand over the sick servant. If Jesus would just give him a word, that was all he needed.

Contrast this centurion's faith with the little faith of Thomas, who was one of Jesus' twelve disciples. The first time the risen Christ appeared to His disciples, Thomas wasn't present. The other ten disciples told Thomas that Jesus was resurrected, but it was eight more days before Jesus appeared to His disciples with Thomas present.

> *"The other disciples therefore said to him, "We have seen the Lord."*
>
> *So he said to them, "Unless I see in His hands the print of the nails, and put my finger into the print of the nails, and put my hand into His side, I will not believe."*
>
> John 20:25

Jesus walked up to Thomas and told him to put his finger into the print of the nails and thrust his hand into Jesus' side and to not be faithless but believing. Thomas fell on his knees and confessed Jesus as his Lord and God.

> *Jesus said to him, "Thomas, because you have seen Me, you have believed. Blessed are those who have not seen and yet have believed."*
>
> John 20:29

Jesus placed a greater blessing on those who "believe without seeing" than those who believe because they have seen. In other words, there is a greater anointing on believing the Word than believing signs and wonders.

Don't get me wrong. I believe in signs and wonders. Jesus used them like a bell to draw people unto Himself and so should we. But the ultimate, the *more sure word of prophecy*, is the written Word of God.

There is a greater blessing on just believing God's Word than there is on believing because of supernatural circumstances. Those who are looking for circumstances to confirm their faith will fail when the strong battles of unbelief come. We have to get our faith so rooted in God's Word alone that we can withstand a hurricane.

Maybe there's a reason the Lord hasn't used an emotional touch to deliver you from unbelief. Maybe it's because He loves you so much that He's trying to help you operate in the highest form of faith — *faith that takes Him at His Word*.

Get Focused

We're all going to think about "something" all day long. Why not choose to think about what God said about you? God says something so powerful in Joshua 1:8. *"This book of the law, this Bible, shall not depart out of your eyes, but you shall meditate on it day and night. Then you shall make your way prosperous and you shall deal wisely and you shall have good success."*

Notice it's when you begin to meditate on God's Word, when you begin to think on the promises of God, that wisdom and success and prosperity come.

So my challenge to you today is to think about what you're thinking about. Examine your thought life regularly. Don't allow Satan to deceive you into living a life of fear and anxiety and worry. Jesus said, *"Which one of you can add one inch to your stature by worrying?"* Nobody can, so don't waste your time doing it.

Learn to meditate on God's Word. Let me encourage you to find at least one Scripture this week that applies to your area of need and dwell on it all week long. If you have to, write yourself a note as a reminder. You can put a note on your refrigerator, on the mirror where you get dressed, and on your steering wheel. But constantly replay that Scripture over and over and over again. Dwell on it. Magnify it. Imagine it. Ponder it.

If you do that, it's going to be impossible to worry. It's going to be impossible to be filled with fear and anxiety. Do you know why? Your mind is renewed and it's focused on the things of God. And God promises to keep you in perfect peace when you do that.

Let's be doers of the Word today. Not just hearers only. Don't say, *Oh, that was a good message.*

No don't let it go in one ear and out the other. You've got to make a quality decision today that you are going to refuse to worry anymore. You've got to refuse to listen to Satan's lies. You're going to cast down those negative thoughts. You're only going to fill your mind with good things, wholesome things, pure things. Not the junk of this world. Constantly meditate, imagine, and think on the things of God and what He says about you—and you'll be well on your road to a victory comeback in the name of Jesus.

Meditation Brings Blessing

All God's blessings take place when you begin to meditate and fill your mind with the promises of God's Word. Do you know what meditate means? It means to ponder, to imagine, to dwell on, to say the same thing over and over again in your mind.

You might be thinking, *I don't know how to meditate.*

Yes you do. You know how to *worry* don't you? Some of us rehearse and replay all the bad things that we imagine *might* happen—we think about them constantly.

What are you believing God for today? You've got to find the Scriptures that apply to your situation and constantly think about them, imagine them, ponder them, and replay them over and over in your mind all week long.

This is how you keep your mind on the things of God. This is how you avoid worrying and being filled with fear and anxiety. The best defense is a good offense. If your mind is totally filled with the promises of God's Word, then when Satan comes to bring those negative thoughts and when he comes to try to get you to believe one of his lies, it's too late. Your mind is already full. There's no room for him. It is filled with the promises of God.

It's Okay To Copy

When I take lessons from a guitar instructor, for example, I become his disciple in learning the guitar. I listen to what he says. I follow his instructions and his example.

Wouldn't it be foolish of me to spend my time and money to learn from that instructor and then out of "humility" say, *Well, I know I could never play like that man. It would be egotistical to even try.*

No, it wouldn't be egotistical to copy that instructor. In fact, it would be foolish not to copy him. After all, that's why I'm taking lessons!

Jesus is my teacher, and I figure if I spend enough time around Him, if I listen to Him long enough, talk like Him long enough and act like Him long enough, I'll eventually be more like Him. I'll experience a victory comeback!

That's really what He was telling us there in John 8. He was saying, *I'm a free man. And if you'll keep on hearing and believing My Word, you'll know the truth and the truth will make you just as free as I am.*

Fearless With the Name

In one of the Apostle Paul's prayers for the church, he stated that God had raised Jesus from the dead and set Him at His own right hand in heaven, *"Far above all principality, and power, and might, and dominion, and every name that is named"* (Ephesians 1:21).

By Jesus' conquest of these principalities, powers, might, and dominion, He obtained His excellent name!

This conquest Jesus made over the devil, sin, sickness, and disease is wrapped up in the name of Jesus. That Name, when we use it, will bring into reality what Jesus has already accomplished in His death, burial, resurrection, and seating on high—in our lives.

I think this is the very reason the devil has fought so hard to keep pastors and teachers from being bold enough to tell us about this power. In fact, the devil is extremely happy that many people do not even believe they have an enemy, (the devil). Many people do not resist bad things, (sickness, poverty, and sin) that come against them because they have been erroneously taught that it was God working something out in their lives.

Colossians 2:15 says, *"And having spoiled principalities and powers, He [Jesus] made a show of them openly, triumphing over them in it [the cross]."*

Believers Have the Keys

In other words, the devil and his demons have been reduced to nothing! It's no wonder Jesus said the believers will cast out demons (Mark 16:17), because He delivered us from the power of darkness. When you understand this truth, and you know that the Name of Jesus belongs to you—you can resist sin and sickness every time!

The Name of Jesus is the key!

Believers need to be using the mighty Name of Jesus and the Word of God far more than we have been—and in every situation in life—especially *before* things get out of hand!

Developing an active confidence in this mighty name is absolutely essential! It's because of a lack of confidence in the Name of Jesus and the Word of God that we have not been living with *fearless faith* that is pleasing to the Lord.

The Word Will Make You Free

Do you know what that truth would do for you? It would make you free! Swindlers couldn't lie to you anymore. They couldn't steal your money by charging you for four tires and only giving you three.

What's more, you'd be free to go on to greater mathematical truths. You could go on to multiplication, algebra, calculus and trigonometry. But as long as you thought two plus two is three, you couldn't put those things to work for you. They wouldn't function as long as you believed two plus two is three, so you would be stuck in that one little place.

I know that sounds like a silly example, but, the fact is, people believe things in the spiritual realm all the time that are just as silly. You'll hear them say things like, *"Well, that's just the way it is in our family, we have heart attacks. We're accident-prone. We all get cancer. You know, like father like son."*

You can go through a thousand healing lines, but if you keep on believing lies like that you will end up bound by sickness. If you don't eventually get in the Word and find out the truth that *"by [Jesus] stripes ye were healed"* (1 Peter 2:24), you'll never really be free.

Jesus Was A Bible Reader

Some people don't seem to realize that Jesus lived by faith. They think that because He was the Son of God, He just floated through life with some mystical, supernatural power we could never have.

Jesus walked by faith—and He got that faith the same way we get it. *"Faith comes by hearing, and hearing by the word of God"* (Romans 10:17). How do you think His mother knew to tell the leaders of the wedding feast at Cana to do whatever He told them? (See John 2:1-11.) How did she know He could solve the problem of no wine?

The Bible tells us He had never done a miracle at that time. Yet He had always lived by faith. He was living by faith when He was just a little fellow of 12 years old saying, *"I have to be about My Father's business."*

Year by year He kept growing in faith, just as He grew physically. He wasn't born a faith giant. He had to develop, just as we do. He said, *"I have many things to say and to judge concerning you, but He who sent Me is true; and I speak to the world those things which I heard Him"* (John 8:26).

Jesus had to be taught. How was He taught? By the Holy Spirit through the written Word!

Luke 4:16 says when Jesus came to Nazareth, *"He came to Nazareth, where He had been brought up. And as His custom was, He went into the synagogue on the Sabbath day, and stood up to read."*

Jesus was a Bible reader! That was His custom. He studied. He meditated. He was trained in the Word of God. He knew the truth and the truth made Him free!

Now more than ever before, it is vital that you and I follow in His footsteps. We simply cannot afford to cast aside our Bibles and go skipping off after signs and wonders.

No! Our Father needs us to grow up in Him. He needs those who will train to stand on the Word and develop their faith so that instead of seeking miracles at the hand of others, they will become the hands that deliver those miracles.

That is training that will change your world!

In the Image of His Love

As born-again children of God, you and I ought to be growing up into the image of Jesus. With every day that passes, we should be walking, talking, thinking, and acting more like Him. Instead of crying in fear about the storms of life that come against us, we ought to be taking authority over them. We should be speaking to the storm like Jesus did and say, *"Peace! Be still!"*

Some people think it's practically blasphemy for us to imagine we could ever be like the Lord.

But the New Testament plainly states that is our destiny.

Jesus said, *"He who believes in Me, the works that I do he will do also; and greater works than these he will do, because I go to My Father"* (John 14:12).

The apostle Paul wrote that we are predestined *"to be conformed to the image of [God's] Son, that He might be the firstborn among many brethren"* (Romans 8:29) and to *"grow up in all things into Him who is the head—Christ"* (Ephesians 4:15).

The apostle John said it this way: *"As He is, so are we in this world"* (1 John 4:17).

As amazing as those Scriptures are, many believers instinctively know they're true and bear witness that they've been born again to be just like Jesus.

God wants to do the same things through us that He did through Jesus!

Some of us have stepped into that on occasion. We've had moments when we experienced the life and power of God flowing through us. But we don't yet live in that place on a day-to-day basis.

What is it that we've been missing? The fullness of God's love.

Practice Makes Perfect

Of course, to complete the process of developing your faith in God's love you must not only allow it to flow to you—but through you to others. As 1 John 4:12 says, *"...If we love one another, God abides in us, and His love has been perfected in us."*

Remember the old saying *practice makes perfect*? That's absolutely the truth. The way to perfect God's love in you is by practicing that love toward other people.

Don't just practice it on the easy ones either. Don't just focus on loving the people who are kind and gracious to you. (The Bible says even outright sinners can do that.) Determine to love those who irritate you and act *ugly* toward you. Purposely love those who have hurt you.

Start by making sure you have forgiven them of any wrong they have done to you. Even if you don't emotionally feel like forgiving them, do it anyway by faith. Say, *Father, I am forgiving this person out of obedience to your Word. I refuse to hold anything against them. Right now by faith I receive from You the grace to love them.*

Then pray for that person. Ask God to help them and bless them. Don't sit around waiting for some kind of supernatural warm, fuzzy feeling to make you do it either. Just pray for them by an act of your will. Ask God to help you see that person the way He sees them.

Faith without action is dead so take the time in prayer to "see" them the way God does. Start by picturing them in your mind and then visualize Jesus coming right up behind them and taking them in His arms. See them totally engulfed in Him. Then pray, *Yes, Lord, that's the way You treated me. You loved me and had mercy on me when I didn't deserve it. Help me do for them what You did for me. Lord, I let Your forgiveness and compassion for them find expression through me.*

You may think you can't do that right now. But I guarantee you if you'll step out in faith, you'll tap into the love of God and find out you can. You'll find that the more you believe the love God has for you and the more you practice it toward others, the more it is perfected in you.

As you keep on developing that love, with every day that passes, you'll grow up a little more into the image of Jesus. Fear will be driven out of your life so you'll start walking, talking, thinking and acting more like Him. The works Jesus did, you will boldly do also…and others will see Him in you.

Whatever is in Your Heart Will Come Out

What you *really* believe is what you *say* when the pressure is on. If you want to find out if you are in faith or not, listen to what you are saying in the privacy of your own home. And know this: Even behind closed doors in the dark of the night, what you say matters.

Malachi 3:13-15 tells us God was listening when His people said, *"What good does it do to serve God? You know, those rich folks down the road don't have any trouble"* (a personal paraphrase). God confronted them about their grumbling. He said, *"Your words have been harsh against me."*

Don't let your words be harsh against God. He is not your problem—He's your answer! Release faith with your words and give Him something to work with.

Don't do what the children of Israel did in Deuteronomy 1:27 either. At the report of giants in the land, they allowed fear to enter their hearts and they began murmuring in their tents. They grumbled, *"Oh, the Lord must really hate us to bring us out of Egypt only to be killed by giants in the land He promised us"* (a personal paraphrase).

God heard the words they were saying in the privacy of their dwelling places, and their words were evil in His sight. The people didn't have faith in what God had promised them, so a whole generation missed out on the blessing of entering the Promised Land.

If you're not getting results, don't murmur and complain. Instead, come to grips with the fact that you may need to change what you're believing and saying. You can't say one thing and reap another. You cannot talk decrease and expect increase. Your words are your sickle. They bring in whatever harvest you have sown. So don't say, *"Nothing's happening."* Instead, say, *"I have it and I'll not be moved until it manifests, in Jesus' name."*

You cannot talk decrease and expect increase. Your words are your sickle. They bring to you what you say.

What's in Your Heart?

Matthew 12:34-35 says: *"Out of the abundance of the heart the mouth speaks. A good man out of the good treasure of his heart brings forth good things, and an evil man out of the evil treasure brings forth evil things."*

Here Jesus is telling us that our words reveal what we have been consistently filling our hearts with. As we fill our hearts with the Word of God and believe it, faith will overflow into our words. Those words filled with faith have power and will affect our circumstances.

Out of the good treasure of our hearts, good things will come forth.

If you don't have good treasure stored in your heart—if you're not believing the right things—you can change what you believe. Simply go to the Word, see what God says about your situation and declare, *That's the way it is. I'm honoring that Word and doing it.* That's how you take the Word into your heart.

Filling your heart with God's Word establishes God's kingdom in your heart. It gives you His words of dominion.

In Matthew 6:22-23, Jesus said: *"The eye is the lamp of the body. So if your eye is sound, your entire body will be full of light. But if your eye is unsound, your whole body will be full of darkness"* (*The Amplified Bible*).

In other words, what you give your attention to is critical.

The entrance to your heart is through your eyes and ears. The "eye" of faith looks at the Word of God instead of the circumstances.

You can have a sound "eye" by following God's instruction:

> *My son, give attention to my words; Incline your ear to my sayings.*
> *Do not let them depart from your eyes; Keep them in the midst of your heart;*
> *For they are life to those who find them, And health to all their flesh.*
> *Keep your heart with all diligence, For out of it spring the issues of life.*
>
> Proverbs 4:20-23

Verse 23 in *The Amplified Bible* says, "Keep and guard your heart with all vigilance and above all that you guard, for out of it flow the springs of life." What we allow into our hearts affects every part of our lives.

Renew Your Mind With the Word

If we spend time in the Word allowing it to flood our hearts, Psalm 119:105 says it will be a lamp to our feet and a light to our paths. But if we are filling our hearts and minds with worldly information—watching worldly television and movies, reading worldly books and magazines—our hearts will not be filled with light. Only by renewing our minds with the Word of God (Romans 12:2) will our hearts be flooded with light.

As you renew your mind with the Word, you learn to think like God thinks and you'll make right decisions—you'll be blessed. That is what Matthew 6:33 is talking about when it says, *"But seek (aim at and strive after) first of all His kingdom and His righteousness (His way of doing and being right), and then all these things taken together will be given you besides"* (*The Amplified Bible*).

If God truly rules in your heart, if He is Lord of your life and you do what He says, then the kingdom of God (His dominion, presence, power, glory and anointing) will continually flow out of you and take authority over the things coming against you. That's God's plan of dominion. Words of authority are words of faith from the heart.

Faith—the Believer's Lifestyle

A lifestyle of faith is the lifestyle of a true believer. Romans 1:17 declares, *"The just shall live by faith."* That passage in *The Amplified Bible* says, *"The man who through faith is just and upright shall live and shall live by faith."*

Faith pleases God because it makes a way for Him to work in our lives. It connects us to His supernatural anointing. Look at Abraham. God promised to bless him saying, "A father of many nations have I made thee" (Genesis 17:5). Though it seemed impossible, Abraham believed God who *"calls those things which do not exist as though they did"* (Romans 4:17). *"He staggered not at the promise of God through unbelief; but was strong in faith, giving glory to God"* (verse 20).

When he agreed with what God said, he saw the promise come to pass. He received the promise because he believed God.

Believers today can walk in the same favor Abraham enjoyed. Galatians 3:29 declares, *"If you are Christ's, then you are Abraham's seed, and heirs according to the promise."* Verses 7 and 9 say, *"Therefore know that only those who are of faith are the sons of Abraham."* And, *"So then those who are of faith are blessed with believing Abraham."*

Don't Quit Believing

It takes faith for the blessings of God to manifest in our lives.

Hebrews 6:12 instructs us: *"Be not slothful, but followers of them who through faith and patience inherit the promises."* God's Word will come to pass in your life if you will put it in your heart and in your mouth. Be patient. Don't dig up your seed with words of unbelief.

Satan comes to steal the Word that has been planted in your heart. He'll try to make you quit. But when pressure comes, recognize the source and the reason. Persecutions and afflictions arise for the Word's sake (Mark 4:15-17). The enemy tries to get you to believe something other than what God has said in His Word.

But don't quit believing! Don't quit confessing the Word. Don't let pressure cause you to speak negative, unbelieving words that give the enemy license to operate in your life. And don't focus on the circumstances or talk about them. Instead, *talk to them.*

Be a faith person—someone who not only says the right things in church on Sunday, but who consistently says the right things all the time. Even in challenging circumstances, a person of faith believes God's Word is true. Even when it looks hopeless, talk the Word.

The things you *continually* say are the things that come to pass in your life.

****

It's Comeback Time!

"Personal Forecast" Strategies To Overcome Set-backs

Pastor Ron Craycraft
Forecast For Life Church

www.ForecastForLife.org

****

90 Personal Forecast Confessions
(Your Personal Prophecies)

Rather than saying how you feel—say what God's Word says about you!

Christians of the 21st century are finally entering a new awareness of becoming more like Jesus. We are discovering the importance of our responsibility to pray and receive the power of God in our lives. We are learning to trust God and His Word rather than our feelings, hurts of the past, or what other people say.

We are learning about speaking God's Word for salvation, healing, protection, abundance, and blessing for our lives and everyone we meet. We are also learning that a negative, doubt-filled conversation—especially with unbelievers—will cancel out our prayer of faith.

Consider this thought: You can help others if you are free from sin. You will pray for others with a passion after God has healed you. You will give generously and make a difference for the poor, after God has made you abundantly prosperous. You can be an encourager, after you have believed God for a miracle.

Use the 90 *forecast* "confessions," on the following pages, to build yourself up, and for encouraging everyone you care about. *(God has given us a way to "escape" and rise above the storms of life—and this is it!)*

For best results—say them aloud!

Personal Forecast Confessions
(Your Personal Prophecies)

- I believe that Jesus took my sins and bore my sicknesses—that He was raised from the dead. Now I am spiritually "born-again" by confessing that Jesus is my Lord and Savior.
  Romans 10:9 and 1 Peter 2:24

- I humble myself, and God exalts me. I cast all of my cares on the Lord, for He cares for me. I am determined to love God with all my heart, soul, and strength, and my neighbor as myself.
  1 Peter 5:6-7 and Matthew 22:37-40

- This Book of the Law shall not depart from my mouth, but I will meditate in it day and night, that I may observe to do according to all that is written in it. For then I will make my way prosperous, and then I will have good success.
  Joshua 1:8

- Lord, I hide Your Word in my heart, so I will not sin against You. I walk in love, even as Christ has loved me.
  Psalm 119:11 and Ephesians 5:2

- I repent and turn away from sin for the kingdom of God is at hand. I lay aside every weight and sin, and run with patience the race that is set before me.
  Matthew 4:17 and Hebrews 12:1

****

- Thank You Lord, for always leading me to triumph in Christ Jesus. I can do all things through Christ who strengthens.
  2 Corinthians 2:14 and Philippians 4:13

- The Lord is on my side; I will not fear. What can man do to me? The Lord is my light and my salvation; Whom shall I fear? The Lord is the strength of my life; of whom shall I be afraid?
  Psalm 118:5 and Psalm 27:1

- I will say of the Lord, "He is my refuge and my fortress: My God, in Him will I trust."
  Psalm 91:2

- I continue to hear and do the Word of God. Therefore it will be as if I have built my life on a rock; and when the storms of life come against me and try to bring me down—I will not fall, for my life is built on Christ the solid rock.
  Matthew 7:24-25; James 1:22

- I can understand and remember the words of Jesus by the teaching of the Holy Spirit. By listening to the silent voice of the Holy Spirit, I can foresee things in the future and know the truth of God's Word.
  John 14:26 and John 16:13

****

- The Holy Spirit helps me when I do not know what to pray. I will pray with the spirit (heavenly words) and I will also pray with the understanding.
  Romans 8:26-27 and 1 Corinthians 14:15

- I am blessed with all the fruits of the Spirit, and the gifts of the spirit (especially prophecy)
  Galatians 5:22-23 and 1 Corinthians 12:1

- By faith, I am filled with the knowledge of God's will in all wisdom and spiritual understanding. God has given me all things that pertain to life and godliness.
  Colossians 1:9 and 2 Peter 1:3

- By faith, I am healed by reading and speaking the Word.
  3 John 2 and Psalm 107:20

- The Lord blesses my bread and takes sickness away from my life. I receive my meals with thanksgiving, and I call it blessed by the Word of God and prayer.
  Exodus 23:25 and 1 Timothy 4:5

****

- I keep the Word fresh in my spirit and soul—it is life to me and health to my body.
  Proverbs 4:20-22 and 3 John 2

- Death and life are in the power of my tongue. I determine to speak only words of life.
  Proverbs 18:21

- I do all of my work excellently and with great prudence, making the most of my time.
  Proverbs 22:29 and Ephesians 5:15-19

- Jesus is the high priest of my profession, therefore I hold fast to it. I have the spirit of faith in Christ; that's the way I believe and speak.
  Hebrews 4:14 and 2 Corinthians 4:13

- I am strong in the Lord and in the power of His might. I have good courage and a strong heart.
  Ephesians 6:10 and Psalm 27:14

It's Comeback Time!

- Jesus took my infirmities and bore my sicknesses—by His stripes I am healed.

  Matthew 8:17 and 1 Peter 2:24

****

- God has given me the measure of faith. I have the God kind of faith.

  Romans 12:3 and Mark 11:22

- Set a guard, O Lord, over my mouth; keep watch over the door of my lips. I let my speech always be with grace, seasoned with salt, that I will know how to answer each person.

  Psalm 141:3 and Colossians 4:6

- Dear Lord, let the words of my heart and the meditation of my heart be acceptable in Your sight, O Lord, my strength and my Redeemer. I am not conformed to this world. I am transformed as I renew my mind to God's Word. I experience the good and acceptable and perfect will of God.

  Psalm 19:14 and Romans 12:2

- Pleasant words are like a honeycomb, sweetness to my soul and health to my bones.
  I will be swift to hear, slow to speak, slow to wrath, in Jesus' Name.

  Proverbs 16:24 and James 1:19

- I am a believer and not a doubter. All things are possible to me. The words of Jesus are spirit and life to me.

  Mark 9:23 and John 6:63

****

- I do not allow the worries of this world or the deceitfulness of riches or the lust of other things to enter into my heart and choke the Word.
  Matthew 13:22-23; Mark 4:19

- I imitate Jesus, copying Him, and following His example, and He leads me by the inward witness.
  Ephesians 5:1 and Romans 8:16

- I study, speak, and obey God's Word day and night, so I am wise, prosperous, and successful.
  Joshua 1:8 and Psalm 1:1-3

- The Lord is my helper, and I will not fear what man can do to me. I am not tormented because all fear is cast out in God's perfect love.
  Hebrews 13:6 and 1 John 4:18

- I have not received the spirit of bondage again to fear, but I have received the spirit of adoption whereby I cry "Abba, Father."
  Romans 8:15

- I find favor and high esteem In the sight of God and man. I trust in the LORD with all my heart, and lean not on my own understanding;
  Proverbs 3:4-5

****

- I am not afraid because God is my salvation and I trust Him. I do not fear, for God has redeemed me and called me by name—I am His.
  Isaiah 12:2 and Isaiah 43:1

- I do not fear nor am I dismayed, because God is with me. God makes me strong and helps me and upholds me with His victorious and righteous right hand.

  Isaiah 41:10

- I study the Word—and the blessings of God come to me and overtake me.

  Deuteronomy 28:2

- I listen to the Lord, therefore, I dwell safely and I am quieted from the fear of evil. I avoid snares because I do not fear man, but I place my trust in the Lord. Therefore, I am safe.

  Proverbs 1:33 and Proverbs 29:25

- I will not fear nor be discouraged, for the Lord my God has set the land before me — I will go up and possess it. I am strong and courageous, delivered from fear, because the Lord my God goes with me. He will not fail me nor forsake me.

  Deuteronomy 1:21 and Deuteronomy 31:6

****

- I delight in God's Word. I am not afraid of bad news, for my heart is fixed, trusting in the Lord. I will not fear, for the Lord my God shall fight for me.

  Psalm 112:7 and Deuteronomy 3:22

- I am strong and courageous, not fearful and dismayed, for the Lord Jehovah is my strength, my song and my salvation.

  Isaiah 12:2

- I walk in the peace that Jesus has left for me, not peace as the world gives. My heart is not troubled neither is it afraid. I do not fear, for it is my Father's good pleasure to give me the kingdom.

  John 14:27 and Luke 12:32

- I will not allow tribulation, persecution, cares of this world, the lust of other things, or the deceitfulness of riches—to take away the Word from my heart.

  Mark 4:19

- I reverently fear the Lord. I respect and honor Him—therefore I do not lack. For the LORD God is a sun and shield to me; the LORD bestows favor and honor to me; and no good thing does he withhold from me because I walk is blameless."

  Psalm 34:9 and Psalm 84:11

****

- When I pray according to the Word of God, I believe I receive and the Lord answers. Then, I am quick to forgive others so my prayers are not hindered.

  Mark 11:24-25

- I do not allow my heart to be ruled by stress or emotions because I trust and abide in Christ Jesus.

  John 14:1

- I am determined to love the Lord with all my heart, soul, and strength, and my neighbor as myself.

  Deuteronomy 6:5 and Luke 10:27

- God is on my side, I will not fear. No weapon formed against me will prosper. Thank You Lord!

  Psalm 118:6 and Isaiah 54:17

It's Comeback Time!

- Lord, I give my attention to Your Word; Incline my ear to Your sayings. I do not let them depart from my eyes; I keep them in the midst of my heart; For they are life to me, and health to my body. I keep my heart with all diligence, For out of it spring the issues of life.
   Proverbs 4:20-23

****

- Greater is He who is in me than he who is in the world. I am more than a conqueror through Christ Jesus.
   1 John 4:4 and Romans 8:37

- As I continue to hear the word of Christ, and remain diligent to *do* the Word, It will be as if I have built my life on a rock: and when the rain descends, the floods come, and the winds try to bring me down; I will not fall, for my life is founded on the rock.
   Matthew 7:24-25

- I will be anxious for nothing, but in everything by prayer and supplication, with thanksgiving, I let my requests be made known to God. The peace of God, which passes all understanding, will guard my heart and mind through Christ Jesus.
   Philippians 4:6-7

- The Holy Spirit has come upon me—giving me boldness and power to be a witness of the good news about Christ!
   Acts 1:8

- I keep my mind stayed on the Lord; therefore I have an abundance of peace.
   Isaiah 26:3

- Lord, I pray that I am strengthened with might by Your Spirit in my inner man—and I thank You that Christ dwells in my heart by faith.

  Ephesians 3:16-17

****

- I am a disciple of Jesus and abide in His words. The Word makes me free.

  John 8:31-32

- Lord, I pray that I be rooted and grounded in love, and will comprehend with all saints what is the breadth, and length, and depth, and height of the most powerful thing that exists.

  Ephesians 3:17-18

- Lord, let me know the very love with which You love Jesus—which passes all human knowledge—that I might be filled with all the fullness of God.

  Ephesians 3:18-19

- Jesus took my infirmities and bore my sicknesses; by His stripes I am healed.

  Matthew 8:17 and 1 Peter 2:24

- The Lord is my light and my salvation; Whom shall I fear? The Lord is the strength of my life; Of whom shall I be afraid?

  Psalm 27:1

****

- I will enter into His gates with thanksgiving, and into His courts with praise. I will be thankful to Him, and bless His name.
                                                            Psalm 100:4

- I will bless the Lord at all times; His praise shall continually be in my mouth. My soul shall make its boast in the Lord; The humble shall hear of it and be glad.
                                                            Psalm 34:1-2

- Lord, I give my attention to Your Word; Incline my ear to Your sayings. I do not let them depart from my eyes; I keep them in the midst of my heart; For they are life to me, and health to my body. I keep my heart with all diligence, For out of it spring the issues of life.
                                                            Proverbs 4:20-23

- This is the day the Lord has made; I will rejoice and be glad in it. I will shout for joy and be glad, and favor God's righteous cause; And I will say continually, "Let the Lord be magnified, Who has pleasure in the prosperity of His servant."
                                                            Psalm 118:24 and Psalm 35:27

- I will bless the Lord at all times; His praise shall continually be in my mouth, My soul shall make its boast in the Lord; The humble shall hear of it and be glad. Oh, magnify the Lord with me, And let us exalt His name together.
                                                            Psalm 34:1-3

****

- I will dwell in the secret place of the Most High and will abide under the shadow of the Almighty. I will say of the Lord, "He is my refuge and my fortress; My God, in Him I will trust."
                                                            Psalm 91:1-2

- The Lord is the Refuge and Stronghold of my life—of whom shall I be afraid? In the day of trouble He will hide me in His shelter; in the secret place of His tent will He hide me.
    Psalm 27:1, 5

- I let the peace of God rule in my heart, and let the word of Christ dwell in me richly in all wisdom, teaching and admonishing others in psalms and hymns and spiritual songs, singing with grace in my heart to the Lord. And I am very thankful.
    Colossians 3:15-16

- Lord, I will meditate on Your precepts, and contemplate Your ways. I will delight myself in Your statutes; I will not forget Your Word.
    Psalm 119:15-16

- The peace of God, which surpasses all understanding, will guard my heart and my mind through Christ Jesus.
    Philippians 4:7

****

- By faith I am healed by reading, meditating, and speaking the Word.
    3 John 2 and Psalm 107:20

- The Helper, the Holy Spirit, whom the Father will send in Jesus name, He will teach me all things, and bring to my remembrance all things that Jesus has said to me.
    John 14:26

- When He, the Spirit of truth, has come, He will guide me into all truth; for He will not speak on His own authority, but whatever He hears He will speak; and He will tell me things to come.
    John 16:13

- I Keep my heart with all diligence, for out of it spring the issues of life. I do not allow my heart to be ruled by stress or emotions because I trust and abide in Christ Jesus.
  Proverbs 4:23 and John 14:1

- Lord, I hold on tight to my hope, because it does not disappoint. The love of God has been poured out in my heart by the Holy Spirit, Who was given to me.
  Romans 5:5

****

- God has not given me the spirit of fear, but of power and love and a sound mind. Your testimonies also are my delight and my counsel.
  2 Timothy 1:7 and Psalm 119:24

- I thank You Lord, that as I continue to hear the word of Christ, and remain diligent to *do* the Word, It will be as if I have built my life a rock: and when the rain descends, the floods come, and the winds blow and try to bring me down; I will not fall, for my life is founded on the rock.
  Matthew 7:24-25

- I am becoming an encourager with my words. I guard my words, and that keeps me from a lot of trouble.
  Ephesians 4:29 and Proverbs 21:23

- I forgive others so my prayers are not hindered. I reverently fear the Lord. I respect and honor Him; therefore I do not lack.
  Mark 11:25 and Psalm 34:9

It's Comeback Time!

- By faith in the Lord Jesus, when I say to this mountain, 'Be removed and be cast into the sea,' and do not doubt in my heart, but believe that those things I say will be done, *I will have whatever I say.*

  Mark 11:23

****

- Death and life are in the power of my tongue, And as I love it, I will eat its fruit. With this truth in my heart, I am becoming the best I can be in Christ.

  Proverbs 18:21 and Philippians 1:6

- As I listen to the voice of the Holy Spirit, I let no corrupt word proceed out of my mouth, but I speak words of edification, that it may impart grace to the hearers.

  Ephesians 4:29

- I have a great High Priest who has passed through the heavens, Jesus the Son of God, Therefore I hold fast to my confession.

  Hebrews 4:14

- I am determined to "Fight the good fight of faith and lay hold on eternal life, to which I have been called and have confessed the good confession in the presence of many witnesses."

  1 Timothy 6:12

- Set a guard, O Lord, over my mouth; Keep watch over the door of my lips. When I feel weak, I boldly say, 'I am strong.'

  Psalm 141:3 and Joel 3:10

****

- Let the words of my heart and the meditation of my heart Be acceptable in Your sight , O Lord, my strength and my Redeemer. By faith I overcome the devil by the blood of the Lamb and by the word of my testimony.
  Psalm 19:14 and Revelation 12:11

- I am determined to let my speech always be with grace, seasoned with salt, that I will know how to answer each person. My pleasant words are like a honeycomb, sweetness to my soul and health to my bones.
  Colossians 4:6 and Proverbs 16:24

- By faith in Christ Jesus, I will be swift to hear, slow to speak, and slow to wrath. Out of the abundance of a good treasure in my heart, I will speak good things.
  James 1:19 and Matthew 12:34-35

- Now thanks be to God who always leads me in triumph in Christ, and through my holy life diffuses the fragrance of His knowledge in every place.
  2 Corinthians 2:14

- Now the Lord is the Spirit; and where the Spirit of the Lord is, there is liberty, But we all with unveiled face, beholding as in a mirror the glory of the Lord, are being transformed into the same image from glory to glory, just as by the Spirit of the Lord.
  2 Corinthians 3:17-18

****

- The Lord is my strength and song. The Lord is my light and my salvation; Whom shall I fear? The Lord is the strength of my life; Of whom shall I be afraid?
  Psalm 118:14 and Psalm 27:1

- Lord, I receive grace and peace multiplied to my life in the knowledge of God and of Jesus our Lord, As Your divine power has given to me all things that pertain to life and godliness, through the knowledge of Him who called me by glory and virtue.
  2 Peter 1:2-3

- Lord, I reflect on Your Word and You give me understanding. You make my words wise. I am committed to learning more and more about You Lord—this makes me wise. This wisdom is a blessing to me and everyone around me.
  Psalm 49:3 and Proverbs 1:5

- I'm created in God's image and likeness. I am a believer and not a doubter. All things are possible to me.
  Genesis 1:27 and Mark 9:23

- I do not count myself to have apprehended; but one thing *I do,* forgetting those things which are behind and reaching forward to those things which are ahead,

  I press toward the goal for the prize of the upward call of God in Christ Jesus.
  Philippians 3:13-14

****

- Thank You LORD! You have promised to watch over Your Word, and I am ready for You to perform Your word in my life. I know the thoughts that You think toward me, LORD, thoughts of peace and not of evil, to give me a future and a hope.
  Jeremiah 1:12 and Jeremiah 29:11

****

Thank you Heavenly Father. I pray that all my victories and blessings in Christ will be for Your glory and honor, for my benefit, and for the benefit of every one I meet, in Jesus mighty Name!

****

Special Note to Readers who are not sure if their destiny is heaven

You *can* be confident that you have a place in heaven when you die.

You might be surprised to know that this confidence is not about becoming religious or doing good works to earn your place in heaven. You should also know that God is not mad at you, and is using every good thing in heaven to reach you—without overriding your free will.

You don't have to be good enough. That's why Christ died for you. He paid the price for you—for *not being good enough.* (None of us deserve God's grace and mercy. God is awesome!)

What's required is a sincere, heartfelt prayer like this: *"God in heaven—I'm not sure about You, and church, and all the rest—but I need Your help and forgiveness. I truly believe that Christ died for me and rose from the dead—and I confess Jesus to be my Lord and Savior. Please fill me with Your Holy Spirit. Amen."*

You may not feel any different, but God has promised to change you on the inside. Your spirit is born again. This is a real miracle in-progress for you—and it starts today! (See John 3:3-17 and Romans 10:9.)

Printed in the United States
207326BV00001B/76/P